ARKANA

R.J. STEWART

THE PROPHETIC
VISION OF MERLIN

R.J. Stewart is a Scot, a musician, composer and author. He has written books and essays on music, folklore, mythology and symbolism, and has a long-standing involvement with western esoteric traditions. He has composed for feature films, television, radio and stage and recorded five L.P. records.

R.J. STEWART

THE PROPHETIC
VISION OF MERLIN

PREDICTION, PSYCHIC TRANSFORMATION, AND THE
FOUNDATION OF THE GRAIL LEGENDS IN AN
ANCIENT SET OF VISIONARY VERSES

WITH ORIGINAL ILLUSTRATIONS BY FELICITY BOWERS

133
.3
Ste

NORTH BAY
DEC 2 0
DISCARDED
PUBLIC LIBRARY

ARKANA

LONDON, BOSTON AND HENLEY

First published in 1986 by Arkana,
an imprint of Routledge & Kegan Paul plc

14 Leicester Square, London WC2H 7PH, England

9 Park Street, Boston, Mass. 02108, USA and

Broadway House, Newtown Road,
Henley on Thames, Oxon RG9 1EN, England

Set in Sabon 10/11pt.
by Columns of Reading
and printed in Great Britain
by The Guernsey Press Co Ltd,
Guernsey, Channel Islands

© R. J. Stewart 1986

No part of this book may be reproduced in
any form without permission from the publisher,
except for the quotation of brief passages
in criticism

Library of Congress Cataloging in Publication Data

Stewart, R.J., 1949-
the prophetic vision of Merlin.

Bibliography: p.
Includes index.
1. Prophecies (Occult sciences)—History.
2. Merline. 3. Prophetia Merlini (Geoffrey of Monmouth)
4. Great Britain—History—Miscellanea. I. Title.
BF1805.S74   1986   133.3   85-10764
British Library CIP data also available

ISBN 1-85063-018-6

Contents

Illustrations

Acknowledgments

No book dealing with the work of Geoffrey of Monmouth should fail to acknowledge J.S.P. Tatlock, *The Legendary History of Britain* (University of California Press, 1950). Tatlock is the most comprehensive study published, and has proved invaluable in the factual preparation of this analysis of *The Prophecies*. A study of the literary development of British prophecies, including those of Merlin, is found in *The Political Prophecy in England* by Rupert Taylor PhD. (Columbia University Press, 1911).

I would like to express my gratitude to John Matthews for drawing my attention to Thomas Heywood's *Chronographical History* of 1641, in which Merlin's prophecies act as a framework for a liberal but painstaking account of British legendary and factual history up to the reign of Charles I. Thanks are also due to Caitlin Matthews and Basil and Roma Wilby for suggestions and reference sources during the preparation of the chapter dealing with Orion and the Pleiades.

Felicity Bowers prepared the original artwork, following my crude sketches. I should also thank various people collectively; those who listened in mild amazement or downright disbelief to my case in support of *The Prophecies* as a meaningful text. Such discussions, over a period of several years, have done as much to clarify the arguments as has the more academic research.

R.J. Stewart
1985

It is quite clear that everything this man wrote about Arthur or his successors, or indeed about his predecessors, was made up partly by himself and partly by others, either from an inordinate love of lying or for the sake of pleasing the Britons.

> William of Newburgh, *Historia* 1190. (Concerning Geoffrey of Monmouth)

In the stead of a large study book, and huge voluminous tractate, able to take up a whole year in reading, and to load and tire a porter in carrying, thou hast here a small manual containing all the pith and marrow of the greater made portable for thee.

> Thomas Heywood, *The Life of Merlin Ambrosius* 1641

Meanwhile Taliesin had come to see Merlin the Prophet who had sent for him to find out what wind or rainstorm was coming up, for both together were drawing near and the clouds were thickening. He drew the following illustrations under the guidance of Minerva his associate.

> Geoffrey of Monmouth, *Vita Merlini c.* 1150

MERLIN'S GIFT

I sit upon a high place
On hard rock;
I look upon a land,
The ring of broken bells,
The song of flown bird,
Anger of dead place,
Murmur of lost people.

No mere love can ease them,
No drug appease their pain,
No sleep heal such wounds.

Not I with my sight
Or harp of hands,
Not plucking strings
Not singing back daylight,
Nor I in the broken tree
The empty nut
Star clouded
On the drawing waiting height;

Nor you, a single child,
Nor any child of blood
Can open terror's eye,
Pluck forth the root
Then stem the deep born giant of the flood.

Up stone and under reach
In earth the warm veins leach
Out dark gold from waiting suns,
Into web-ways for your gift;

Friends hand alone shall shape
The drowsy stone
Becoming joy to heal.

Distant is the time of which I speak,
Open is the heart on that wild day
To all pain, all voices of the weak,
All victims of the wheel.

Yet distant is come close
Upon this hilltop chair;
There is no moment of unwoven space
I may not touch,
No measure of unspiralled time
You may not share.

(R.J. Stewart, 1983)

Introduction

Between 1965 and 1984 over eight thousand books of both fiction and non-fiction were published on Arthurian subjects. This staggering figure was augmented by plays, radio and television productions, feature films, a perennially successful musical, a rock musical on ice; the output reached such proportions that one successful film, 'Monty Python and the Holy Grail', was an outrageous parody of the genre.

Serious works are still emerging from publishers in a steady stream; an author researching modern literature upon Arthurian themes would be hard pressed to keep up-to-date.

While this flood of material, both academic and popular, has been flowing forth into the libraries, theatres, and homes of the western world, there has arisen a renewed interest in the deeper psychological, magical, and mystical aspects of Arthurian lore.

In this book I propose to deal exclusively with specific aspects of the character of Merlin, particularly an almost unknown ancient work: *The Prophecies of Merlin*. To approach this subject, some of the basic roots of Merlin are laid bare, enabling us to see his significance as a motivator of the western psyche.

Merlin comes from an area beyond the reach of a merely psychological interpretation, however, and his magical or otherworldly powers are traditionally said to be derived from his parents: a mortal mother and an immortal or otherworldly father. We may see in this tale several levels of interpretation, which are considered in depth in later chapters, but for introductory purposes we may regard the mother as the human psyche, while the father is a power or mode of consciousness outside the psyche, which may at certain times be joined to it.[1]

In such a context, we shall approach *The Prophecies*. The liberal modern attitude to astrology, prediction, and journalistic workings of various prognostications (the most famous

1

being those of Nostradamus) tends to obscure the hard fact that prophecy was a serious matter to our not so distant ancestors, and that it was not limited to mere prediction of events or tendencies. In the wake of the authority of orthodox religion, prophecy is often assumed to be the sole property of bearded and venerable Biblical characters, or of exotic individuals such as Nostradamus[2] or in more recent times Madame Blavatsky.[3]

The truth is quite different, for there is a strong tradition of native British prophets and prophetesses, which is ultimately derived from a Celtic and perhaps pre-Celtic psychology and metaphysics. The two popular seers mentioned above both partook of this source in its broadest European manifestations, for it transcends specific modern nationalistic concepts while remaining a western school of inner development. So much emphasis is placed upon Blavatsky's 'Eastern masters', or Nostradamus' 'Black magic', that eminently western seership of both is passed over. A highly intellectual development of the same seership was undertaken by the remarkable Rudolf Steiner,[4] whose influence in practical fields such as education, health, music, and mental welfare now permeates many areas of our culture.

But the originator of this seership was Merlin, and his visions are virtually ignored by modern researchers and occultists, as by psychologists. This ignorance is sadly extended to later and more historical figures, such as Thomas The Rhymer,[5] who influenced the development of European literature and made some very accurate verse prophecies, or the Reverend Robert Kirk,[6] who investigated the second sight, translated the Bible into Gaelic, and is rumoured (like both Merlin and Thomas) to have disappeared into Fairyland.

Looking into the origins of Merlin is more than a literary exercise. His first biographer was probably Geoffrey of Monmouth, writing in the twelfth century but drawing upon earlier written and oral traditional sources.[7] The character of Merlin is so enwrapped in literary accumulation that recourse to basic root material is sometimes surprising. There are, for example, traditions of Merlin quite apart from the Arthurian legends; traditions which seem to derive from a distant motif of the relationship between human consciousness and the land, handed down through the dream-like vehicle of oral lore from a far distant culture.

The Prophecies, incorporated by Geoffrey in his great book *The History of the British Kings*, are strange and often incomprehensible. But they are no more obscure than those of Nostradamus, and are less political and literary in content. Scholars suggest that *The Prophecies of Merlin* are a body of poetry or visionary material from oral wisdom traditions active in Geoffrey's day.

As chronicler of mythical history, Geoffrey drew upon earlier texts and directly upon his own considerable intimacy with Welsh tradition. Before Geoffrey there was very little in writing about the Arthurian cycles, but after his *History* and the shorter *Prophecies* and *Life of Merlin*, Arthurian material blossomed into the full-blown literary variants familiar today in translation and in derivation.

Despite the ancient and magical character of *The Prophecies*, they do not feature in the literature of the modern revival of esoteric lore, and apart from a small number of translations, hardly feature as literature either.[8] Yet they are a fully developed esoteric text, a manual of psychology and metaphysics which is central to western transcendental traditions. Furthermore, they illuminate certain key issues within Arthurian lore, for they reveal the means whereby Merlin acquired his vision, his power, and his ultimate relationship with the land of Britain.[9]

One of the more obvious reasons for the relative obscurity of *The Prophecies* is the simple and sad fact that westerners are still rather unaware of their own inner or transcendent traditions. Even those who have pioneered the resurgence of such traditions seem to draw heavily upon orthodox and eastern sources and authorities, compounded with interpretations attuned to the doctrines of modern psychology.

Second, we must understand that the native wisdom material is available only in translation from ecclesiastical Latin, medieval or period Welsh, Irish, Scots or early French. Very few of us can be scholars of such breadth as to study the texts directly in each tongue; even if we could, there are severe problems in translation due to corruption, editing, dialect, conventional usage and many other uncertain aspects.

Set against this problem of sources, is the undeniable fact that translations and re-writings from the Middle Ages to the present day have fired the popular imagination, and that Arthur, his Knights, The Quest, and Merlin, are all potent psychological images. They are also effective and powerful magical images.

In the following chapters, I have made use of the translation by J.A. Giles[10] although I have also studied other translations listed in the Bibliography, and have on occasions examined original Latin and native language texts, but without any pretension to linguistic scholarship.

The material is primarily poetry, and even the broader prose of The History of the British Kings is a poetical and mythical work rather than a straight historical book. The various translations employed, therefore, are chosen as much out of poetic preference as for their linguistic or scholarly achievements.

Fortunately the literary and detailed study of the texts is not our main concern, for a key to The Prophecies should reveal some coherent and readily applicable conclusions regarding the method and the structure of the whole sequence, rather than the placing or translation of various obscure words.

By attempting to find the heart of The Prophecies, we find the heart of the seer, traditionally said to be Merlin. The historical existence of Merlin cannot be proven, yet as with the existence of Arthur, there is some suggestion that historical and mythical characters have merged inseparably. Esoteric tradition suggests that there has been more than one Merlin, and that each incorporates the power and wisdom of his predecessors. This is a most ancient and consistent tradition indeed, directly comparable to that of the divinity of kings, or the ancestral power descent of the pagan hierarchies, maintained until very recent historical times in the genealogies learned by rote in Celtic cultures.[11] The traditions of some occult schools go so far as to suggest that Merlin is linked to lost Atlantis, as a carrier of wisdom to new horizons, fleeing the ruin of corrupt civilization.[12]

This is precisely the theme of Geoffrey's History, where Britain is founded by Brutus, whose ancestors fled from the sack of Troy.

Cataclysm features strongly in *The Prophecies*, to the very end of ordered solar or zodiacal time. Little wonder that such lore should be linked with the classical and occult tradition of a lost continent; they are harmonically, magically, and psychically, the same event. Historical correlation is irrelevant, for all falls are the fall of Atlantis.

If, in the main text of the book, I am discovered writing of Merlin as if he is a 'real person', I write of his human nature derived from his mother; if I am suspected of treating him as an otherworld power, it is as a result of his paternal origins.

Within our own psychological structure Merlin is what is often referred to as an 'archetype'; he typifies wisdom from a source that is not personal or human, yet applied to humanity both individually and at large. This was his role in the guidance and original creation of Arthur, and this is his role in the stimulation of our imaginations and the creation of our hopes to survive or even prevent our own Atlantean style of holocaust.

The accuracy of the individual elements of *The Prophecies* is dealt with in our later chapters, but at this stage it seems apt to refer to the rather detailed descriptions of what appear to be nuclear radiation effects, somehow inextricably linked to the morality of the people who dare to create such forces and use them in war.

Luxury shall overspread the land, and fornication shall not cease to debauch mankind. . . . Famine shall then return, and the inhabitants shall grieve for the destruction of their cities. . . . In those days shall the oak trees burn and acorns grow upon lime trees . . . the Severn sea shall discharge through seven mouths, and the river Usk burn for seven months. Fishes shall die with the heat thereof, and from them shall be engendered serpents. (*The Prophecies of Merlin*)

The aim of this study is not to provoke doom and depression, but to show that at some distant moment the seer had foreseen strange powers and endings of cycles, yet at the same time had encapsulated within his vision the very means whereby this inevitable process could be routed through the human psyche in such a way that it was balanced and purified. In this sense, *The Prophecies* hold a secret illumination of the

Quest for the Grail,[13] which was replete with both great danger
and great joy.

Merlin is not a cure for our collective ills; he is not a placebo
or 'hidden master' who will appear and set the world aright.
Such beings, by the inherent nature of our world, cannot really
exist. There are dynamic methods hidden within the story of
Merlin, and perceptive maps of the hidden levels of the human
psyche. We can use Merlin to revitalize our imagination, to
catalyse our individual and collective awareness in a way that
reaches deeper than academic research and further than
pleasant fiction.

As *The Prophecies* are Merlin's most concentrated and
valuable gift to us, his descendants, living in what he may have
classified as the Fourth Age from the creation of the worlds, we
may seek his secrets within them. Perhaps it is offhand to
suggest that we 'use' Merlin as if he had no true identity; but
this issue of identity may only be proved if we succeed in
awakening him from sleep, a Mystery which will be further
revealed as we progress through the key to *The Prophecies*.

To some, Merlin will always be a literary and remote figure,
a being employed to link and explain certain facets of
Arthurian lore in the manner of the old theatrical *deus ex
machina*. To others he will be the allure and the fantasy of
power to manipulate mere mortals. Yet Merlin is not any kind
of god, and his manipulations of the Arthurian realm were
clearly failures due to unbalanced forces. If we reach far
enough into the collective depths of our old lore, the fruits of
our ancestors' creative imagination, we will find a being who is
human enough to seek a manifested realm of order and justice,
yet who is sufficiently inhuman to make such a realm out of
magical genetics, illusion, and strange powers of foresight. If
we reach deeper still, we find a prototype of the magician or
shaman who becomes attuned to the land, and becomes one
with it in a voluntary sacrifice. In these legends, Merlin is
enchanted by a female power, who causes him to merge with a
flowering hawthorn tree. This and other periods of disappear-
ance represent cycles of withdrawal from the active psyche,
both individual and collective.

If the ferment of the last fifteen years of Arthurian material is
an accurate sign, then we may expect Merlin to reawaken soon,

though not as a wise elder who will appear in our midst and give instructions. During his period of withdrawal into the UnderWorld, where knowledge is given and powers realigned, Merlin will have accumulated some new developing consciousness, something which may filter through to us all if we apply to his key image and his root vision that has lasted through the centuries.

Our personal response may be on any number of levels, from superficial entertainment to a far-reaching and shattering change of awareness.

PART I

The power in theory

Magical and psychic origins of the
traditional *British Prophecies*

CHAPTER 1
Merlin, maker and tutor of kings

In some sources other than Geoffrey we find Merlin as a tutor to the young King Arthur. He causes the hero-king to be born through a magical and astrological conjunction of forces, expressed physically as Uther Pendragon and Ygraine the wife of Gorlois of Cornwall.

After creating the opportunity for conception through enchantment and shape changing, Merlin takes the resulting infant away into seclusion, where he protects him and imparts his early education. It is Merlin, also, who arranges the fostering of the secret king, a typically Celtic motif, and who subsequently advises Arthur after his ascent to the British throne. It is Merlin who makes the Round Table, which leads to the final Quest.

Sequences of this sort may be fruitfully interpreted upon several levels, and it is far from sufficient to read such a pattern as the paradigm of a perfect realm and ruler, advised by esoteric wisdom. Indeed, Arthur's realm, created and supported by ancient powers and genetic magic, was inherently flawed. The expression of this flaw, Mordred, the physical offspring of incest between Arthur and his sister, is no idle moralistic fantasy; it reveals the working of potent forces breaking through into an unbalanced generation.

Before we ask whether or not Merlin has any possible value as a tutor of kings today, we should first consider the levels of his record as teacher and manipulator, and reveal some of the loosely disguised implications of his career.

One of the most obvious and most repeated errors of occult or esoteric groups and movements has been to identify too closely with the nationalistic elements of traditional wisdom. Such mythic and dynamic structures may be kingdoms of unbalanced force if they are aroused without a spiritual or ethical awakening within each individual.

The first level, therefore, upon which we must meet Merlin the Tutor, is within ourselves. The old story of the breeding and birth of the infant, his seclusion and foster-training, and his final claim to the rightful throne, may be successfully applied as an analogy of the inner development of any man or woman.

In such a role, Merlin is that part of the psyche which acts out of will and wisdom, seeking to combine otherwise disparate elements of the entity into a fruitful union. That this fruition is gained through enchantment or illusion is no coincidence, for the nourishment of the inner being, the infant that will in time claim full union of consciousness and power, is obtained through the controlled use of imagination. In the traditions of both east and west, the process is stimulated by a collection of instructional verses, tales, chants or songs, all of which are insubstantial and illusory by the standards of hard fact, but which have hidden potency and purpose. This is one meaning of the shape-changing by which Uther, the potent male dynamic power, obtained access to Ygraine, the seductive and fruitful female power.

The method was clearly laid out in many alchemical texts from the Middle Ages to the eighteenth century, and was rediscovered from oriental sources in the twentieth century by the examination of works such as *The Secret of the Golden Flower* (Jung and Wilhelm).

We find in Merlin's role as maker and tutor of the created king a deep understanding of the human psyche, not from a merely intellectual or analytical standpoint, but in connection with the hidden powers of the human being attuned to the environment. The Waste Land of the later stages of the Arthurian cycle is not merely an analogy of the personal psyche, but of the physical environment deprived of the fruitful harmony of balanced powers of life and death.

As with many wisdom-tales, the progress of Merlin's plans is spiral. The conception and birth of Arthur, and his ascent to the throne of the Land, is one complete cycle of realization, which may be worked within each individual seeking a full and harmonized consciousness with a complete magical and physical through-line of energy.

The subsequent career of the young king is a further turn of the spiral, revealing the same forces as they operate through a social or group awareness. It is in this interplay that the first elements of failure occur in the old tales. Merlin makes the Round Table as a symbol not only of the order of the knights, but of the Wheel of Life and Change, with its perilous elements of change and spiritual insight. This leads us to the third turn of the spiral, the Quest for the Grail, a further expression of the realization cycle, but upon a spiritual level.

If we seek to apply to the image of Merlin within our imagination, we should first individually attempt the conception and inner rebirth epitomized by Merlin's creation of Arthur. This new consciousness, like the alchemical child or philosopher's stone, should be nourished and developed until it takes its rightful place as ruler of a harmonized mind and body. This is no small task, but it is not quite as daunting or impossible as it first appears.

In eastern terms, this achievement alone is often sought as the primary aim of inner development, usually under the protecting umbrella of a guru, or school of religion. The western spiritual and magical paths, however, seek to feed the changes back into the mass imagination, where they will act as a catalyst upon the general consciousness, no matter what the ultimate form of expression may be. It is this second stage of group catalysis that is often confused with crude and ignorant nationalism, and may be open to abuse. The wisdom of Merlin is one of the methods of utilizing these energies correctly.

In the terms of the old traditional lore, how may a new order be created out of the social and environmental chaos which ferments through our culture?

If any individual or group dares to take upon themselves the archetypical images and patterns of the Arthurian myths, they will polarize and amplify each and any inherent weakness or corruption within themselves. The failure of Merlin's designs seems clear in historical terms; no similar attempt has yet succeeded, nor is it ever likely to succeed, due to the cyclical nature of our world.

Yet Merlin's work led to the Grail Quest, which had three successful candidates. Each of these candidates epitomizes a level of consciousness that exists within us all. They could not have gained the Grail without the cycles set into motion by Merlin, even though he himself has disappeared into the

UnderWorld by the later stages of the Quest.[1]

The three who gain the Grail are Galahad, Perceval, and Bors. Galahad is the spiritual and pure movement of being within the human entity; Perceval is the mediating power of the Innerworlds; Bors is the material return and promise to the outer world.

In the Quest, the first vanishes into the Unknown, the second takes up the interior kingship of the Grail Castle, while the third bears witness of the experience to the court of Camelot.[2]

If the modern meditator or magician applies to the Merlin of the innerworld, he or she may set in motion the forces symbolized by the stories of Merlin, Arthur, and the Quest for the Grail. But it is only by merging the Three Enlightened Ones *as one being* that this Quest may truly be made manifest in our world.

In ancient times, a far-reaching attempt was made to create such a being by genetic magic, and Merlin partook of this wisdom in action, in his creation of Arthur. As we have already discussed, Merlin himself was the product of magical union between a human woman and an otherworldly being. The myth is a recurring one, wherein a woman is visited by a lover who she may not look upon in his true form. Conversely, no man may look upon the true face of the Goddess and live, for she must remain veiled, as in the ancient temples.

Just as personal rebirth is mirrored by group rebirth, in the cycles described above, so may we apply magically as individuals to the group pool of energies attuned to the image of Merlin. By so doing, we draw upon these energies to change ourselves.

This is an essential difference, often misunderstood, between eastern and western systems of inner development; in western magic an application to collective awareness is employed to trigger psychic and spiritual rebirth, often in a dramatic and cathartic manner. In eastern systems there is a preference for gradual all-embracing development, often with a hierarchical emphasis such as that which runs through Christianity in its Roman and later forms.

Christianity is essentially an eastern religion in the context of its approach to the human psyche, and this may be one reason for its failure in the western world. We should not, however, take this as an exclusive difference between east and west, for schools such as Tibetan and Zen Buddhism, which are both allied to chthonic earlier cults, employ the same direct methods of transformation as those of the western esoteric traditions.

It is, of course, the inevitable corruption of hierarchical power (Arthur's incest with his sister) which begets the doom of the Kingdom, and which prompts the Quest.

At certain stages of the cycles of development and decay, Merlin seems to stand aside, or disappear. He initiates a new potential golden age with the birth of Arthur, but is absent during his fostering. He helps Arthur gain the Throne and to rule wisely, but cannot prevent the doom of the begetting of Mordred.

He organizes the Round Table, and hence the Quest, yet it is the seeking of the Grail that accelerates the closing of the Arthurian age. At the present time, folklore gives us both Arthur and Merlin sleeping, in the blessed isles, or in the hollow hills, both being representations of the UnderWorld of the Celts.

From an esoteric and magical viewpoint, it should be realized that Merlin's apparent periods of imprisonment and inactivity are actually more important than his known actions. If we reconsider the old tale of Merlin's enchantment by Nimue, a sorceress or priestess of the Dark Goddess, we find that it contains the seed of the old transformative magic of the UnderWorld. When Merlin is asleep or imprisoned, he is separated from our surface group consciousness. During these periods, which bear no relationship to serial or historic time, Merlin is under the power of the Goddess of Taking, and it is his absence from our consciousness that allows the breakdown of static and potentially corrupt hierarchies or structures of society. We could just as easily observe that it is not Merlin that sleeps, but ourselves.

Upon re-emerging from the dark UnderWorld phase, the prophet is equipped with new levels of wisdom, and these are the seeds of group consciousness for a coming age. This concern with ages and their modes of consciousness is apparent in *The Prophecies*, as we shall see in later chapters.

Merlin emerges from the shadows shortly after a period of collapse, and initiates fresh areas of focused harmonized awareness, both in the individual psyche, and in the social expression of a collective consciousness.

It is indicative of the mass imagination on a broad predictive level that a fresh upsurge of interest in the Arthurian lore and in Merlin has occurred within the period of the last fifteen or twenty years. This has arisen hand in hand with presentiments of holocaust, and the death of an age of mankind. Yet the lore of Merlin as expressed through Arthur is not necessarily comforting, and *The Prophecies* themselves seem to suggest the very disasters that modern westerners most fear.

In the image of Merlin our collective need is realized, not just that of the individual seeker after magical lore, but of the entire people and their land or lands. This is not a religious experience, but a matter of wisdom and knowledge. Merlin is undoubtedly pagan in his origins, yet he creates the bridge between the old magic and the true Christian mysteries. In times of stress and collapse, we may seek to draw him from his abode in the UnderWorld.

Merlin is the meeting of Light and Dark, born of a fallen angel and a mortal woman. He is, in fact, the concentrated and finely focused consciousness of an enlightened being who has chosen not to escape to paradise, but to remain and serve an ultimate end. During his long retirement into the depths, we grasp intuitively that Merlin has acquired the wisdom necessary for the forthcoming age, and that this wisdom may be seeded into the imagination of each and every one of us if we ask for it in the right manner.

CHAPTER 2
The breath of prophecy

Thereupon he straightway burst into tears, and drawing in
the breath of Prophecy, spake, saying . . .

Having considered the background of the character of Merlin,
we may now turn to *The Prophecies* themselves. Despite the
garbled and often incoherent aspects of the material which,
curiously, is a valuable asset in terms of altered consciousness,
there is a clear pattern and system of metaphysics within the
text.[1]

The Prophecies form one book of *The History of the British
Kings*, but are clearly a separate work, and were set out as such
by the chronicler, Geoffrey of Monmouth. Geoffrey's collection
and publication (in the limited sense of copies made for reading
aloud to an elite but illiterate noble audience) of both Merlin's
Life and *Prophecies* were extremely popular with their
medieval patrons.[2]

The inclusion of *The Prophecies* within the larger scope of
the *History* is not a matter of padding out a manuscript with an
already popular theme, but is a subtle mirror image of British
mystical lore encapsulated within the mythical *History* that
represents such lore in outward expression.

We meet *The Prophecies* as a highlight of Merlin's famous
conflict with King Vortigern, and his foreseeing of the struggle
between native Britons and incoming Saxons. This is a prelude
to the advent of King Arthur.

The prophetic sequence mirrors in miniature and cryptic
form the overall project of the entire *History*, to run from
ancient times to the last of the 'British' Kings, Cadwallader.
This important pattern of reflection will be reconsidered later in
our analysis. *The Prophecies*, however, move beyond
Geoffrey's medieval period into the most distant future, and
reach symbolically to the 'end of Time'.

It is impossible to offer a detailed study of the entire
prophetic sequence, though this has often been attempted for
work such as the writings of Nostradamus. To undertake such

a task would require a separate and very different book in its own right, and such a work would never be complete in a rationalist sense. There are other significant reasons for omitting a line by line correlation of Merlin's prophecies. Despite the problems, we can find some close affinity between both the structure and the content of *The Prophecies*, and the western esoteric tradition of the UnderWorld or Otherworld initiation and journey.

The Otherworld experience is a theme that runs through western initiatory lore, and forms a keystone of our mystical consciousness. Its ramifications stretch from humble folk tales of adventures in Fairyland, to fully developed visionary flights and voyages under the earth or across the sea, by heroes, saints, or seers.[3] *The Prophecies* can only be approached in the light of this theme and its traditional initiation, for they derive from a cultural ambience in which the Otherworld adventure was well known. Indeed, the *History* could only have been understood by people who recognized the many Otherworld themes that it incorporates; the themes which were part of the cultural heritage of the Christian Normans via their combined Viking and Celtic origins. Beyond this level, relished by the aristocracy as heroic justification of their dubious pedigrees and royal rights, lay another mythical layer which was accessible to the native Celts through its many puns and allusions to Welsh or British language and lore.

The shortest possible summary of this Otherworld initiation would be thus:

> *An individual is transported magically to an Otherworld, which is the origin of all life and death and power. In this Otherworld certain events occur in specific sequence, culminating in a vision of a magical Tree, the fruit of which brings both wisdom and prophecy.*
>
> *During this Journey, the initiate communes with the Ancestors, a tradition derived from the most primitive Celtic roots, the cult of the dead. Finally, the prophetic vision vouchsafes a sequence of insights, some of which are predictive, while others are unutterable in normal language.*

If we respect the weight of evidence from traditional tales, early manuscripts, and folklore up to the present period, and compare this with classical and anthropological evidence in a balance of ancient literature and modern science, then *The Prophecies* can only be a sequence of visions arising from an Otherworld Journey.[4] In this respect, *The Prophecies* are not a quaint and confused sample of Welsh folklore or proto-literate vision, but an important record of a transformative tradition that may be re-evaluated with each successive century. They give us a great deal of information about western magic, mystical experience, and the interplay between myth and history.

The value of prophetic material is subtle, and is not necessarily in the predictive element alone. It is not the details of perception, such as symbols, characters, sequences and correlations that really matter, but the resonance of the act of seership. This act creates and sustains a heightened awareness, and generates a transforming power within the individual psyche.

This is nothing more than a complex way of describing the resonant effect of poetry or visual art, where the insight of the creator is attuned to a specific form, which recreates an echo of that insight in the reader or perceiver of the work of art. Music acts in a similar manner, but with a broader and often deeper level of response. But not all art is prophetic.

Traditional prophecies, from sources that are not fabricated from literary style or political expediency, should be experienced as whole entities. The shape and effect of the whole is of greater importance than the units from which it seems to be assembled. A very simple test of this law may be made by reading aloud from the translations given in Part II. Although the content may seem like nonsense at times, it has that hairraising and blood-tingling effect beloved of all true artists and poets. We may not know in instant intellectual terms what such words and images do to us, but we feel that they do *something*.

To set out a detailed interpretation or corroboration of a set of prophecies is to miss their true worth. Any analysis that attempts to nail down the content of prophecy is inevitably a failure; no matter how well it may define or identify parts of the sequence related to factual history, it cannot satisfy our need for a deeper insight into the prophetic power itself.

Predictions are established by historical hindsight, sometimes through very dubious juggling and speculation. True prophecy should not be confused with prediction, for not all prophetic utterances are limited to statements of future events. The Hebrew prophets, who derived their powers from a similar but not identical tradition to that of Merlin, were mainly concerned with inspiring a backsliding people to attune to their developing tribal god. They were spiritual disciplinarians rather than soothsayers, and had such a potent effect upon both their culture and ours, that we are still suffering from it to the present day.

It is significant that the Hebrew prophets and their subsequent Messianic tradition have helped to polarize an unbalanced male-orientated society in the west, while our own native prophets such as Merlin, Thomas Rhymer, Michael Scot, all derive their power and prophecies from a female innerworld archetype.[5]

The true power of prophecy is multifold; it does not aim at simplistic accurate prediction; such results are considered to be side-effects. A seer does not know the events to which his or her utterances will be enchained by future generations; such events cannot be truly known in the instant of prophecy, for they may take a variety of potential shapes, none of which crystallize until they emerge within the group consciousness, the popular imagination. It is from this consciousness, in traditional esoteric teaching, that events are expressed into time, space, and interaction.

Despite the obvious factor of unknowing, there are always a number of details within any utterance that become clear to the seer. We can find this precise element in *The Prophecies of Merlin*, and will return to it shortly. The recognizable items in a prophecy use a symbolic language known to the seer, and this language acts as an interface between group awareness, and the transcendent cognition which seems to fly beyond time.

In the case of the Hebrew prophets, the subtleties of language and allusion are well known, and we should understand that there are many elements in the Merlin text that would correlate material familiar to the medieval mind in a manner similar to the correlations and cross references between orthodox Biblical prophecies. Such material is embedded in tradition, rather than in literary commentary or manuscript.

A few simple facts often become clear to a seer at the instant of emerging from the prophetic trance. It is as if the consciousness has grabbed a few random items from the stream of energized cognition and pulled them back into the regular intellectual framework. In *The Prophecies*, for example, we wade through a sea of obscure utterances to emerge into clearly defined and ordinary prediction and far-seeing. This concerns the fate of the despicable Vortigern.

'Flee thou from the fire of the sons of Constantine, if flee it thou mayest! Even now are they fitting forth their ships, even now are they leaving the coasts of Armorica and spreading their sails upon the deep. . . .Two deaths await thee, nor is it clear which of the twain thou mayest escape first.' (Evans, 1912)

At this point in *The History*, we have actually left the corpus of traditional prophecies. Merlin has emerged from his trance, and makes predictive and factual statements. He knows not only certain details of Vortigern's potential future or futures, but also news of distant events. All of this more accessible material comes after the true prophecy; it is the winding down or aftermath of the prophetic resonance or afflatus. Not all of this predictive matter is couched in poetic or symbolic language; it is straightforward in comparison to that which has gone before.

Despite the fact that this new chapter is Geoffrey of Monmouth's stylish way of leading us out of traditional lore and into the mainstream of his mythical-historical plot, it demonstrates the esoteric teaching regarding prophetic powers and their effect upon the individual psyche.

First the ferment of the power; then the predictions and the far-seeing are a relatively trivial after-effect. It is in this respect that prophecy or the Otherworld seership differs substantially from popular clairvoyance. Although Geoffrey may have concocted Merlin's factual statement for literary reasons, it would not be presuming too much to suggest that he was familiar, even if at second-hand, with the insight itself. When we remember that the second-sight was so common in the day of Doctor Johnson that it could be purchased with a gift of tea, how much more widespread was the sight and the deeper function of prophecy in the Celtic races of the twelfth century?[6]

Nor is any of this unknown today, for a similar effect is found in the records of modern occultism, where ritualists often report that the most easily accessible contact from the inner-worlds or planes occurs at the close of a ritual, and not during its height. Once again we are encountering the psychic after-effect of energized consciousness, stimulated through ritual work.

In meditational or mystical experiences, the moment of enlightenment is followed by the detailed exposition of the light; the slowing of the rate of awareness as the mind returns to its regular and conditioned functions.

Experienced practitioners often report that they experience a pre-encounter, described traditionally as 'rising through the planes', but this rather pedestrian method seems to play less part in the prophetic and Otherworld experience. In some schools this rising becomes a lengthy basic training, often to the exclusion of all genuine inner experience.

It would be ridiculous to claim that all elements of Merlin's *Prophecies* (or any others) are couched in a fully translatable symbolic mode. Prophecy is invalid if it does not hold to paradoxical and enigmatic patterns. This enigma is not, however, the result of intellectual contrivance except in forged or faked prophecies, or in games with words for entertainment. The paradox derives from a level of consciousness wherein perceptions are unified with understanding. This instantaneous merging of object and subject generates the illusion of predictive value, or 'seeing through Time'.

The unifying consciousness does not truly transcend time and space, as is often suggested, but causes them to coalesce within the perception of the individual. All systems of metaphysics or transpersonal psychology aim to hit this instant of coalescent consciousness. As previously separate streams of awareness merge, they burst into an inner flame that illuminates the psyche and reveals vistas hitherto unimagined.[7] In the most effective systems, this enlightenment is combined with an arousal of the fundamental energies within the physical body, hence the appearance of the mysterious archetypical women in the myths of Merlin, Arthur, and the Quest for the Holy Grail.[8]

It is this transcendent and fundamental female power that

underpins the Otherworld experience, and which is woven subtly but inextricably into the Arthurian legends. We often assume that because Merlin had a daemon or fallen angel for his father, because he manipulated the birth and development of King Arthur, that he is an exaggerated stereotype of male wisdom.[9] This is quite wrong, for his power is derived from an ancient goddess whose particular key motif is that of the Weaver or spider, to whom we shall return shortly.

This relationship is an expression of the basic laws of polarity which apply to all changes of energy, from physical electricity to the flow of consciousness within the psyche.

In the Introduction we met Merlin as the product of a human mother, she being a symbol of the psyche. The male power was active on an inner level, and Merlin's father is a symbol of transforming energy from another world or plane. When Merlin himself becomes the male innerworld archetype, we establish a threefold relationship. In the outer world is the individual or collective psyche, the human symbolic female; in the world of inner nature that lies behind and within our collective consciousness, is Merlin, the being combined of human and non-human parents; and beyond him, in the Otherworld, is the Goddess, completing and balancing the flow of power. She appears in the legends in various guises: the Nine Maidens who tend the Cauldron of Inspiration, the enchantress who seems to seduce Merlin and entrap him in a glass tower or hawthorn tree, the Three Dark Queens who bear Arthur to Paradise, The Lady of the Lake.

It is this female power that catalyses the Otherworld prophetic power, and in the Scottish magical ballads of 'Tam Lin' and 'Thomas Rhymer', she is the formidable Queen of Faery. This queen is no gossamer and tinsel confection, but a passionate and dark beauty who rides a great horse; she can bless and curse, and gives most precise magical instruction to those who dare approach her.

One such candidate for her affection was Merlin, and in *The Prophecies* she appears as Ariadne, the goddess of the thread. In very primal Celtic symbolism this female power is found sewing or weaving a silver thread, not as a token of passive male-dominated domesticity, but as the creator and destroyer of life, and of each individual life woven into her fabric. It may

be significant that Geoffrey has chosen to call this goddess
'Ariadne', in the typical fashion of adopting a classical title
when the native name would be meaningless to the reader or
listener. The myth of Ariadne has another fascinating parallel
in English history, which we shall touch upon later,[10] and
although her original name may have been lost by the twelfth
century, this primal goddess figure remained rooted in the
common imagination.

The resurgence of interest in Merlinic or Arthurian keys to
human consciousness is closely linked to a strong feminizing
and rebalancing urge. This is inevitable, for the symbols of
Merlin are derived from a female divine power, while those of
orthodox Christianity have usurped or denied that power.

When we experience militant feminism at one extreme and
a reversion to various forms of goddess-orientated worship,
magic, and mysticism at the other, we are feeling the effects of
Merlin's new awakening in the consciousness. The goddess has
always been with us, but we have contrived to ignore her or
reject her to our peril. It is not the Goddess who comes awake
in our changing times, but the mediating factors of the
collective imagination, filtering her illimatable power through
to our imprisoned and deprived personalities.

We shall return to the Goddess as Ariadne when we analyse
the climax of *The Prophecies*, but before reaching this climax,
we can consider the structure of the sequence, and its hidden or
partly hidden magical symbolism.

CHAPTER 3
The inner structure of The Prophecies: *I*

There are a number of definable elements within a genuine prophetic sequence, and most of these have nothing to do with prediction of events.

The Prophecies of Merlin, filtered through the grand plan of Geoffrey's chronicle and mythical *History*, are our most important western primitive example of the prophetic elements woven into a vehicle for consciousness. By primitive, we should not understand the text to be crude or ignorant, for like all primitive traditional sources it is extremely sophisticated and complex.

As has been suggested, a very fruitful source of experiment is to take ancient native poetry (in translation) and apply it for meditational and invocatory purposes. This is, after all, a time-hallowed method employed within orthodox religion and literary occultism, where prayers and invocations from the east or Middle East are regularly translated, paraphrased, and often misapplied.

It is often more effective to use verses from the fragments of Welsh, Scots, Irish, and early English material that embodies ancient transcendent traditions of metaphysics and magic. To use old symbols in this manner is not to succumb to quaint antiquarianism or 'Celtic twilight', but to develop a method of by-passing corrupted lines of contact or consciousness within the imagination. It is, poetically, the way of the Mother rather than the way of the Father. The Mother, however, has several faces, and in the prophetic tradition of the west we meet her most potent aspect.

By the reflective power of magic in operation, a successful venture with one key section of the Mysteries may lead to the ability to unlock the whole body from within its hidden chamber.

The text which remains to us from medieval times is

undoubtedly corrupt in the literary sense. It has errors of transcription, interpolations, additions, and omissions.[1] Yet none of these matter greatly from a magical or psychological viewpoint, for most of *The Prophecies* are intact, including the vital passage of the final vision.

As Geoffrey of Monmouth was re-establishing a set of lines or verses that had been upheld by an oral tradition, we should consider the astonishing tenacity and conserving function of such traditions.[2]

Oral traditions are known to hold details accurately, after their own fashion, for centuries. Our main sources of knowledge of ancient Celtic lore are actually medieval or later in date; but they compare so effectively, so sympathetically, with classical and archaeological evidence, that scholars assert their origins to be far older than the extant written variants.[3]

This traditional accuracy or retentive conservative quality must be kept firmly in mind when reading translations of Geoffrey's books. He has merged literary style, classical and traditional symbolism, with a well defined tradition of his own Welsh or Breton people, into a subtle vehicle for a transcendent key to the hidden aspects of the psyche. Yet there is no proof that Geoffrey himself was a practitioner of occult or mystical arts; he was a creative chronicler of living traditions. The depth of his books, which are usually regarded as frivolous nonsense, is derived from the depth of the ancient traditions which they reinstate. Geoffrey's own position within the church-ridden society of his day precluded any notoriety as a magician.[4]

In this respect, he is different from other historical figures who are known to have actually practised the same or similar magical traditions, such as Thomas the Rhymer or the later and more popularized Nostradamus. We shall never know if Geoffrey was overshadowed by the archetype of Merlin as he wrote, or if he, like many others, had partaken of that Otherworld initiation that made him more than human but less than divine.

Geoffrey himself has made personal excuses in a time honoured manner, for he tells us that his work is only a Latin translation of an ancient book set in the British tongue, brought out of Brittany for him to peruse and make available to a non-Welsh-speaking audience.[5] He also includes a large number of rather cunning puns on Welsh words in his Latin, giving more than one level of meaning to any tale, sentence or phrase. While there is no proof that Geoffrey was a so-called 'Initiate', he was clearly employing lore which derived from pre-Christian symbolism, from pagan sources which can be reasonably linked to both Druidism and the older goddess worship.

The elements of the lore set out in *The Prophecies*, whatever their source, may be interpreted as sevenfold. These seven elements have a further fivefold linear order, and relationship between the two is shown in Figure 1.

The seven primary elements may be expressed as a vertical axis of ascending or descending order, which is a long established system used in basic magical tuition. There is no suggestion, incidentally, that one level or unit is superior or more powerful than any other; in this our model differs from many similar expositions in esoteric studies that apply ortho- dox hierarchical concepts to metaphysics.

The seven levels are modes or expressions of awareness which are available to the seer; they are closely interwoven, and react upon one another. (The silly practice, in popular occult books, of using hierarchies to compel lesser powers to obey plays no part in the western traditions no matter how great its spurious literary and orthodox religious accumulation. The inner powers are there to be experienced, not compelled through fear and ignorance.)

Following the diagram, we may define the levels of *The Prophecies* as follows:

1 SPIRITUAL (Religious)
2 ASTROLOGICAL (Astronomical)
3 MYTHOLOGICAL (Trans-personal)
4 POETICAL (Riddling)
5 MAGICAL (Practical)
6 PREDICTIVE (Suggestive)
7 HISTORICAL (Pseudo-historical)

The seven elements are merged tightly, with Prediction playing only a seventh part. Any detailed dissection of the text, aiming to establish a solely historical or factual basis for interpretation, can only be superfluous and misleading.

The Prophecies are the fruit of a system of magic, with a

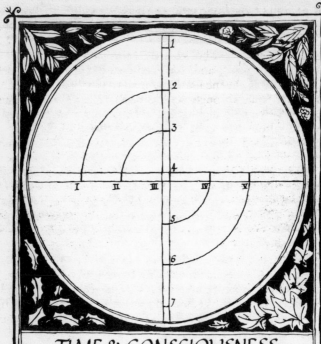

TIME & CONSCIOUSNESS

VERTICAL KEY	HORIZONTAL KEY
1 *Spiritual*	I *Pre-Historic*
2 *Astrological*	II *Heroic*
3 *Mythical*	III *Chivalric*
4 *Poetical*	IV *Transformative*
5 *Magical*	V *Apocalyptic*
6 *Predictive*	
7 *Expressed Historical*	I *Proto-Historic*
CONNECTIONS	II *Roman-Celtic/Welsh Saxon,*
	to 9th or 10th century approx.
I *Pre-History-Astrological* 2	III *Medieval period*
II *Heroic-Mythical* 3	*to 18th century*
III *Chivalric-Poetical* 4	IV *19th century*
IV *Transforming-Magical* 5	*to 21st century*
V *Apocalypse-Predictive* 6	V *21st century*
7 *Historical-Spiritual* 1	*to distant future*

potent pattern of symbolic modes. This interwoven structure is in itself an enchantment or spell, wherein the impact of the whole may change consciousness in an effective manner. The garbled and difficult text becomes transformed in the context of a magical operation, and has mind-suspending properties similar to those of the meditational mantram, or the Zen koan. This function runs through several medieval and anonymous works, and is strongly highlighted in the apocryphal traditions which offer alternative variants of the Christian mythology.

The disregarded nonsense, the incomprehensible rubbish from the fringe of cultural and religious evolution, is the open secret, the final hiding place of the Mysteries. What is particularly significant in *The Prophecies* is the absence of Christian orthodox interpolation or dogma. Unlike the great Grail legends the transforming powers and the predictions do not have a religious resolution, at least not in an orthodox sense.

This absence of Christianity, in an era redolent of the Church, is in itself a prime indicator of two aspects of the text: its pagan origin, and its inherent sanctity. There is no more certain suggestion of the genuine preservation of a prophetic or magical work than that it has been retained more or less intact without rationalization.

In primal cultures the poem or inspired chant is the literal vehicle of divine consciousness flowing through the bard, seer, or seeress. We find this concept stretched to extremes in orthodox Hebrew religious practice, and perpetuated in Christianity for political reasons, where the sacred texts were edited and falsified repeatedly by a worldly hierarchy.[6]

In modern application, which we shall discuss in detail later, the researcher has the difficult task of suspending disbelief sufficiently to attune to the symbolism. If this suspension is carried too far, we fall into the silly state of modern alternative cultism, guru-worship, spiritism and the like, which actually lead us away from the Quest for the Unknown. It is for this reason that effective esoteric traditions and teachers play down the value of prediction, clairvoyance, psychic healing and other peripheral but valuable talents, for they are only valid after the deeper realizations and changes of consciousness have been made.

In *The Prophecies* we can certainly trace some accurate prediction, either through hindsight on Geoffrey's part as chronicler, or through our own rationalization and intellectual appreciation of subsequent history. If we look at the developing order of the text, however, we find a framework of chronology that stands out sufficiently to merit study. The predictions are in a pseudo-historical order, just as the larger work of *The History* is in a similar order, though completed only up to the last 'British' King. *The Prophecies* extend far into the future, including our own future. The order of the sequence is of more significance than the degree of predictive accuracy. It is this order that defines the horizontal axis of our Figure 1.

1 PRE- or PROTO-HISTORY
2 'WELSH VERSUS SAXONS'   (i.e. Celtic, Roman, and on to the ninth/tenth century)
3 INVASIONS AND INTERNAL CONFLICTS (medieval to approx. eighteenth century)
4 MODERN HISTORY   (nineteenth to twenty-first century)
5 DISTANT FUTURE   (to the potential end of our Time cycle)

A reading of the full translated text will give the reader plenty of opportunities to discover the Five Ages for his or herself, but they are not of equal length within *The Prophecies*. Transitions are sudden and understated, as in the change from section 4 to 5, described below. Additionally, the points of transition may vary slightly from reader to reader, not in a factual or detailed logical dispute over content, but in the sense that the transitions from Age to Age are partly dependent upon the psyche of the reader or listener. This harmonic relationship is shown in our diagram, and is common to all metaphysical or transcendent wisdom tales, songs, epic poems or mystical teachings.

In modern psychotherapy a reflection of this process is well known, for there are no hard and fast divisions of the individual consciousness, only general maps and symbolic links and barriers which may be broadly applied in practice.[7] The flexibility of mercurial quality is revealed in alchemical texts also, where the operations are repeated and yet change harmonically; in ritual lodge or temple practice, the ancient method of altering the superficially 'real' order of the physical symbols with each new initiation is yet another statement of this transcendent truth.

The Five Ages are by no means the only way of dividing the text, and are not offered as the ultimate fine division or definition. Any diligent researcher will be able to sub-divide the five sections suggested into events, shorter time periods, and patterns of cultural and social transition. The finer the lore is chopped, however, the less accurate it becomes.

The Five Ages are harmonically attuned to the middle five divisions of our vertical axis, the modes or hierarchies. This relationship is more important to the mystic or magician than the details of manifestation, for when the harmonic relationship has been brought alive within the psyche, the growth of outward-developing details is seen in a new light. This altered perspective is not a flight from specifics into vague generalities, as is often suggested, but the growth of a new and applicable set of values, by which the products of reason, logic, cause and effect, are seen to be just as 'true' as ever, but of a radically different order of reality to that previously retained. An obvious analogy is found in modern physics.

As much of the ambience of *The Prophecies* is astrological, we may restate the graphic key as an astrological key (Figure 2) which shows the Planets identified with the Ages and the Modes of Consciousness.

In an astrological exposition, the discovery and symbolic integration of the more recent planets (Uranus, Pluto, Neptune) fits extremely well with the final Vision of Merlin. While he does not specifically tell us that new planets will be seen, or rather that existing planets will be made visible by developing exoteric science, the qualities assigned to these planets by astrologers of a later age are clearly stated in the drama of the final Vision. This raises the under-emphasized and little discussed topic of the esoteric insight into the structure of the Solar System, for it was from Astrology that stalwarts of science such as Kepler and Newton derived the modern astronomy.[8]

The esoteric teaching on this subject is quite different, for it advises us that the planets actually appear as a result of changes of awareness. Logically this is absurd, yet astrologically it

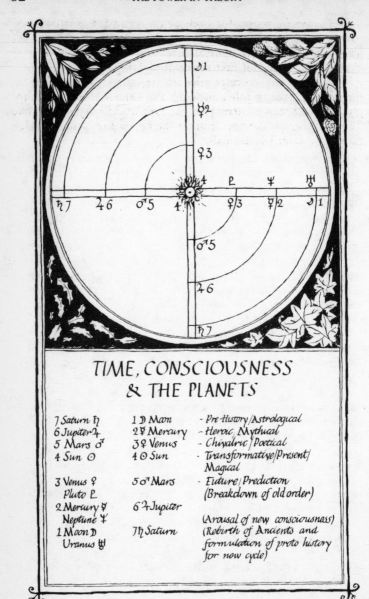

TIME, CONSCIOUSNESS & THE PLANETS

7 Saturn ♄	1 ☽ Moon	- Pre-History/Astrological
6 Jupiter ♃	2 ☿ Mercury	- Heroic/Mythical
5 Mars ♂	3 ♀ Venus	- Chivalric/Poetical
4 Sun ☉	4 ☉ Sun	- Transformative/Present/ Magical
3 Venus ♀ Pluto ♇	5 ♂ Mars	- Future/Prediction (Breakdown of old order)
2 Mercury ☿ Neptune ♆	6 ♃ Jupiter	(Arousal of new consciousness)
1 Moon ☽ Uranus ♅	7 ♄ Saturn	(Rebirth of Ancients and formulation of proto history for new cycle)

makes symbolic sense, for each of the extra-Saturnian planets corresponds to elements of consciousness and changes of planetary (Earth) development that have arisen shortly after or close to the period of first scientific sighting.

These Planetary correspondences are, in fact, allowed for on the ancient 'Tree of Life', although this primarily mathematical glyph only became current in the late Middle Ages, and like *The Prophecies* derives from a much earlier source which cannot be traced historically.[9]

CHAPTER 4
The inner structure of The Prophecies: *II*

For the stars of heaven and the constellations thereof shall
not give their light: the sun shall be darkened in his going
forth, and the moon shall not cause her light to shine.

Isaiah XIII, 10.

The Prophecies, and to a certain extent the greater expanse of
The History, are an expression of an ancient model of the
psyche and the originative spirit, both individually and
collectively. As such they should not be treated credulously,
and we would be quite mistaken to assume that every page
revealed inner wisdom or perceptive intuitions into our own
psychic structure in the modern sense.[1]

Historically this could not have been the case, for the
detailed Mysteries of the ancient Greeks and Romans, or the
oral learning of the native Druids and other Celtic cults, had
long been suppressed by the development of political Christianity.[2] Whatever psychological and magical teachings were
communicated among the ancients, they were not available in
direct and concentrated form to the chroniclers of the tenth to
twelfth century. Before examining *The Prophecies* further, it is
essential to reconsider their perspective within the medieval
common imagination.[3]

Geoffrey was a widely literate individual, yet he includes
many items from native oral traditions, even to the extent of
The Prophecies which contradict, in several places, the
reasoned political-religious attitude which he has written into
the *History*.[4] To one familiar with the contemporary chronicles,
or with the Classics, and with the Bible itself, numerous
literary parallels arise; there is no doubt that Geoffrey used
these consciously, even if, like many medieval authors, he tends
to paraphrase quotations from memory.[5]

The great majority of the recipients of the *History*, and the mass of the general population, would have been totally ignorant of the sources of literary parallel. While Kings are known to have had Chronicles read or recited to them,[6] and the concoction of such books was considered politically expedient to confirm the spurious claims of the Norman nobility, the classics and the Bible were not commonly known, due to general illiteracy of any language. We must picture, therefore, a people ranging from the aristocracy down to the peasant or slave, in which none of the literary parallels was known, nor had they ever been known in any direct form. The practice of reading from Latin chronicles (which were translated into both Norman French and Welsh within a fairly short period of seventy years from the appearance of Geoffrey's *History*) may be regarded as a downward filtering of literary and otherwise unknown influences, reserved for the learned members of the Church, but gradually beginning to break out into general use.

This expansion, which was soon to flourish in the poetry of Wace, Chrétien de Troyes, Marie de France, the Tristan romances, the anonymous Quest of the Holy Grail and Death of King Arthur, was not the sole source by any means. It met and merged with a great store of imaginative material preserved actively within the common consciousness, represented by oral traditions, or as Geoffrey calls them 'jocular tales' or 'common report'.

In the case of Merlin, we have evidence from both Geoffrey and from Gerald du Barry[7] that oral traditions and bodies of prophetic lore were common. When we find parallels within *The Prophecies*, Isaiah,[8] the *Pharsalia*,[9] the Sibylline Oracles,[10] and Thomas Rhymer and Nostradamus, we are emphatically not meeting a combined series of literary allusions, borrowings or plagiarisms.[11] We are, in fact, encountering a common inner experience, which expresses itself in an enduring, if chaotic, form.

In the ballad of 'Thomas The Rhymer', Thomas being in many ways a Scottish and historical Merlin, we find the lines:

> For forty days and forty nights
> He wade through red blood to the knee,
> And he saw neither Sun nor Moon,
> But heard the roaring of the Sea.[12]

As in the final vision of *The Prophecies*, or several Biblical sources, the dissolution is a vision both intimate, personal, and universal.

In primitive initiations, the candidate experiences a lesser death, through fasting, drugs, or induced trance. The classical Mysteries were said to reveal the sight of 'the Sun at midnight'[13] and the powers of Hades or the UnderWorld.

There is an element within our awareness which attunes to the concept of dissolution, not as mere wanton destruction, but as the death that brings a new and greater life. This death and re-birth formed the core of the ancient Mysteries, no matter what their cultural origin, and it is this central vision that we find in *The Prophecies of Merlin*. In the first part of this chapter, a visual key was introduced which presented the elements of *The Prophecies* in an idealized or archetypical relationship.

It is not necessary for Geoffrey to have had such a map directly in mind, although neat correspondences were central to the medieval world-view. The harmonic relationship is a natural occurrence, stemming from a prehistoric conceptual model of existence[14] which reached intellectual heights in the ancient civilizations, and which was perpetuated with the various cosmological models from the Middle Ages through to the present day.[15] The model exists within the human consciousness, and is reflected in our attitude to natural phenomena, the solar system, and the distant stars.

Other significant elements in *The Prophecies* may be summarized as follows:

(a) Poetic style, similar to that of religious chants, and possibly modelled (in Geoffrey's Latin version) on the Psalms.
(b) Totem beasts, including anthropomorphic and theriomorphic characters, and composite animals.
(c) Tree symbolism, often combined with animal symbolism.
(d) Moral or ethical criticism of behaviour, linked to cause and effect through time.

Each of these four areas of symbolism or attitude is typical of pagan religion, not excluding the psalm-like poetry.[16] We cannot suggest any specific religion, but the symbols are found repeatedly in the material that holds British or Celtic mythology.[17] Some of the visionary keys are similar to those which were associated with 'witchcraft' from the late medieval period onwards, but by this we should understand a mixture of dissociated practices, all of which were condemned by the orthodox Church, with no implied cohesion or historical continuity.[18]

The continuity appears from within the symbolism itself, but not as a cult that was preserved intellectually. That such symbolism and associated prophecies in general were still venerated is made clear by the attitudes of Geoffrey, Gerald du Barry, and other medieval authors. To accept such lore outright might smack of heresy, yet it was undeniably sought after, learned, written down, and generally kept in circulation. We find this apparent paradox to an even greater extent in the Grail legends, where some highly unorthodox concepts are embodied in a persistent series of tales which were neither acknowledged nor banned by the Church.[19]

Similar prophetic and poetic lore is found in native sources from Ireland, Wales, and Scotland.[20] In this context it is significant that the Merlin verses in Geoffrey's work are often pan-Celtic and nationalistic. Common action between Wales and Brittany, Scotland and Ireland, is predicted; a romantic concept which has never succeeded due to the independent and fiery nature of these races. Merlin predicted that Ireland would only be conquered in the distant future; to the present date his words seem to hold true, as dissent against English rule has never ceased.

Nationalism is another identifying feature of primal prophecy; such lore was set out in highly nationalistic or tribal cultures, and the more subtle unity of seer and land tends to express itself in a type of nationalism, particularly to the modern reader who cannot separate national identity from politics. To reach a clear understanding of *The Prophecies*, or of any similar material, we should make a distinction between nationalistic politics and the mystical and deep rooted union between human beings and the land. Most occult writings of any value, from ancient to modern, contain a mixture of both; the second being a foundation upon which the first is often perilously assembled.

It is this patriotic and rather contrived motive that is supposed to prompt Geoffrey to his writing of the *History*; from Brutus first King of the Britons, to Cadwallader son of Cadwallo. In this he followed Nennius, whose *Historia Britonum* reached from Adam to the eighth century; and Gildas, whose *Liber Querolus* reached from Rome to the sixth century. Geoffrey's work extends from the fall of Troy to the seventh century. A similar mythical history is mentioned by Henry of Huntingdon, as having been recited to Henry I in 1128. This also stated that the fall of Troy provided the early inhabitants of the land, in this case, France.[21]

FIRST AND SECOND AGES

Returning to our graphic key to *The Prophecies*, we can find the first two Ages on the horizontal axis (Pre-History/Heroic) in the broader tapestry of *The History* itself, while the Second Age opens *The Prophecies* with the words:

> Woe unto the Red Dragon, for his extermination draweth nigh: and his caverns shall be occupied of the White Dragon that betokeneth the Saxons whom thou (Vortigern) hast invited hither. But the Red signifieth the race of Britain that shall be oppressed of the White. Therefore shall the mountains and the valleys thereof be made level plain and the streams of the valleys shall flow with blood. (Evans)

The earlier period or Age is that of the Fall, rationalized as we know from medieval sources in both Britain and France as the Fall of Troy. Irish legend has similar records of arriving peoples,[22] and in esoteric tradition this theme is linked to the story of the fall of Atlantis. The first historical references to Atlantis are in Plato's *Timaeus* and *Critias*, but the tradition is widespread regardless of the specific name of the fallen or sunken land or city.[23]

This pre-historic phase in traditional history is attuned to astrology or astronomy, in which the actions of dimly remembered characters are frequently linked to the long term movements of the starry heavens. In the esoteric traditions, the Atlantean fall is linked to the generation or invocation of a stellar power which proved destructive beyond all bounds of control; and this wild star occurs at the opposite end of our temporal axis, with the apocalyptic vision.[24]

Symbolism of this sort fell into disuse in the late nineteenth and early twentieth century, when it became the property of religious cranks and frauds. Yet the post-war period from the bombing of Hiroshima and Nagasaki has brought a literal realization of such a horror into our world. It is no longer a ridiculous motif that is supposed to terrify us into giving money to a religious cult; it is a sober and indisputable fact. The atomic explosion, which is star-power, creates a disruption analogous to that described by the old seers. While they may have experienced this as a psychic dissolution, we have materialized it into the destruction of matter and life: thus proving the seemingly absurd predictions to be true.

THE THIRD AGE

The Pre-Historic/Astrological Age and Mode merge almost imperceptibly into the Heroic/Mythical stages. As each period is a harmonic of the preceding one, they reflect one another. *The History* contains a retrospective view combining tradition, history, and a certain amount of propaganda and wishful thinking, right up to the Third Age, Chivalric/Poetical. This is Geoffrey's own position in serial time, and it is the point where the horizontal and vertical lines of the visual key intersect.

The Historic and Poetic consciousness merge in the author, Geoffrey, who in a small section of his work re-assembles the words of Merlin. It is the section dealing with Geoffrey's own Age that naturally contains most examples of wishful thinking and expedient writing. Nor can we tell whether or not any of this material was genuinely predictive from an earlier source. We can, however, apply ourselves to historical correlation of material subsequent to Geoffrey's authorship, though some interpolations have been discovered by scholars in the Geoffrey text.[25]

Once again, it should be emphasized that the historical correlation is of less importance than the symbolic material itself. A key image may not only be an oblique reference to

some lost political cause, but may also be a magical image or
source for meditation in its own right. Thus riddles such as
'The shape of commerce shall be cloven in twain; the half shall
be round' are easily interpreted as referring to a contemporary
coinage problem of Geoffrey's own period, but the procession
of symbolic beasts, planets, trees, and combats, which are met
with in the second part of *The Prophecies*, demand a less
superficial consideration. Nor is it certain that such symbolism
has been applied intellectually in every case. A historical
example from as recent a date as 1745 may be valuable as an
insight into the curious merging of myth and history.

The modern vistor to Traquair house in Peebleshire,
Scotland, will find a pair of tall wrought gates, firmly chained
shut. These are the famous Bear Gates, surmounted by the
Stewart Bradwardine family arms, the Bear. The closed gates
are said to be the result of a vow at the time of the Jacobite
uprising in support of Charles Edward Stuart, that since the
rightful king had passed through, they would remain shut
until he sat upon the throne. And shut they have remained,
the Stewart family even display photographs of the members
of the Hanoverian (usurping) Royal Family standing *outside*
the gates. This story would be nothing more than amusing
minor history, if we did not know that the Bear was one of
the symbols of the mythical King Arthur, whose legend came
from Wales/Brittany, and that the Stuart dynasty had
emerged as cup bearers to earlier kings, from Brittany. Both
Stewart and Stuart are variants of the word steward.

Thus a portion of the old Arthurian symbolism was given
factual expression, no doubt through the vehicle of nationalistic fervour and political inclination.

The digression is merely to show that myth and history are
not in any way as separate as we might like to think, and that a
merging of the two is natural to poetical material such as *The
Prophecies*. It is important that we remove our study of such
works from the purely literary and factual correlations, for only
this way will they truly come alive.

FOURTH AND FIFTH AGES

From the period contemporary to Geoffrey, the text becomes more obscure and chaotic, though we can detect certain possible correlations that guide us loosely through the Fourth to Fifth Ages of the graphic key.

It is the last or Fifth Age which is of relevance to the study of *The Prophecies* as an esoteric text in keeping with earlier and subsequent prophetic works.

After a lengthy sequence of visions involving shamanistic or visionary elements the seer makes a sudden transition into the Fifth Age, and describes a zodiacal revolution, leading to the end of known time and ordered creation. As is often the case with such texts, the transition is understated, but it clearly occurs from the line:

> Root and Branch shall change places, and the newness of the thing shall be as a miracle. (verse 88)

This is the vision of the inverted Tree, which plays an important role in ancient transformative psychology. In relatively modern Cabalistic symbolism it is the Reflected Tree of Life, but this has so frequently been intellectualized into a token of imbalance and evil that it is difficult for us to grasp a clear picture of it through contemporary esoteric literature.

In *The Prophecies*, however, its appearance is similar to that UnderWorld Tree encountered by Thomas Rhymer, or to the inverted tree met in mystical experiences which reverses the order of comprehension. It is also the Celtic magical tree frequently encountered in early tales, such as that of Peredur, who sees a tree half of green leaves and half of flames, thus revealing the secret nature of ordinary phenomena.

> On the bank of the river he saw a tall tree; from roots to crown one half was aflame and the other half green with leaves. (Peredur Son of Evrawg, trans. J. Gantz)

As the Fifth Age is the last of the harmonic divisions, it holds both the apocalyptic and predictive consciousness, as shown by the interconnections in our Figure 1. On the time scale established in the interpretations of *The Prophecies* this corresponds to the twenty-first century initially, but soon leaps to the end of the solar system, and thus the end of our collective and individual Time cycles.

In the typical cyclical manner of magical texts, this last section is the most significant and, paradoxically, it is the very primal key to the entire prophetic power. It is from this last section of *The Prophecies*, and from the preamble that leads up to the first prophetic sequence inspired by the appearance of two Dragons from within the Earth, that we learn most about Merlin, his powers, and their relevance to our own spiritual, psychic, and physical relationship with the inner and outer worlds.

CHAPTER 5
Merlin and Vortigern

The Prophecies are usually regarded as an insertion, placed in the heart of Geoffrey's rambling narrative; they are almost an embarrassment to the literary scholar, as so much of their content cannot be deciphered by the usual critical methods.

Before *The Prophecies* start, Geoffrey elaborates upon the theme of King Vortigern and his Tower, drawing from earlier sources and from an established oral tradition. In the light of this setting, *The Prophecies* are not a clumsy or difficult addition, but a very logical result of the allegory of the Tower. Geoffrey has not, in fact, used *The Prophecies* to break up his *History*, but has used the *History* as a massive setting for the jewel of the prophecies.

To appreciate this fully, we must first realize the number of cross references between the *History* and the early parts of *The Prophecies*, in which they confirm one another in a manner that must have been delightful to the medieval mind. This mutual confirmation seems rather contrived to the modern intellect, and often misleads critics into assuming that *The Prophecies* are mere concoctions of plagiarism and wishful thinking, mixed with downright nonsense. If, however, we regard *The Prophecies* as a fore-runner of the *History*, we realize that Geoffrey is writing in the time-hallowed manner of the author on magical and esoteric traditional themes; taking a highly concentrated symbolic sequence, and opening it out for purposes of elucidation and a wider audience.

Before examining the text of *The Prophecies*, we must include their immediate setting, the story of Vortigern's Tower.

VORTIGERN'S TOWER

After usurping the throne of Britain, perpetrating various

43

outrages and murders, Vortigern allies himself with the barbarous Saxons. These dubious allies make free with the land, and like ravening wolves, begin to take over.

History of the Kings of Britain Book V, Chapter XVII

At last he had recourse to magicians for their advice, and commanded them to tell him what course to take. They advised him to build a very strong tower for his own safety, since he had lost all his other fortified places. Accordingly he made a progress about the country, to find out a convenient situation, and came at last to Mount Erir, where he assembled workmen from several countries, and ordered them to build the tower. The builders, therefore, began to lay the foundation; but whatever they did one day the earth swallowed up the next, so as to leave no appearance of their work. Vortigern being informed of this again consulted with his magicians concerning the cause of it, who told him that he must find out a youth that never had a father, and kill him, and then sprinkle the stones and cement with his blood; for by those means, they said, he would have a firm foundation. Hereupon messengers were despatched away over all the provinces, to inquire out such a man. In their travels they came to a city, called afterwards Kaermerdin, where they saw some young men, playing before the gate, and went up to them; but being weary with their journey, they sat down in the ring, to see if they could meet with what they were in quest of. Towards evening, there happened on a sudden a quarrel between two of the young men, whose names were Merlin and Dabutius. In the dispute Dabutius said to Merlin: 'You fool, do you presume to quarrel with me? Is there any equality in our birth? I am descended of royal race, both by my father and mother's side. As for you, nobody knows what you are, for you never had a father.' At that word the messengers looked earnestly upon Merlin, and asked the by-standers who he was. They told him, it was not known who was his father; but that his mother was daughter to the king of Dimetia, and that she lived in St. Peter's church among the nuns of that city.

Chap. XVIII.—*Vortigern inquiries of Merlin's mother concerning her conception of him.*

Upon this the messengers hastened to the governor of the city, and ordered him, in the king's name, to send Merlin and his mother to the king. As soon as the governor understood the occasion of their message, he readily obeyed the order, and sent them to Vortigern to complete his design. When they were introduced into the king's presence, he received the mother in a very respectful manner, on account of her noble birth; and began to inquire of her by what man she had conceived. 'My sovereign lord,' said she, 'by the life of your soul and mine, I know nobody that begot him of me. Only this I know, that as I was once with my companions in our chambers, there appeared to me a person in the shape of a most beautiful young man, who often embraced me eagerly in his arms, and kissed me; and when he had stayed a little time, he suddenly vanished out of my sight. But many times after this he would talk with me when I sat alone, without making any visible appearance. When he had a long time haunted me in this manner, he at last lay with me several times in the shape of a man, and left me with child. And I do affirm to you, my sovereign lord, that excepting that young man, I know no body that begot him of me.' The king full of admiration at this account, ordered Maugantius to be called, that he might satisfy him as to the possibility of what the woman had related. Maugantius, being introduced, and having the whole matter repeated to him, said to Vortigern: 'In the books of our philosophers, and in a great many histories, I have found that several men have had the like original. For, as Apuleius informs us in his book concerning the Demon of Socrates, between the moon and the earth inhabit those spirits, which we will call incubuses. These are of the nature partly of men, and partly of angels, and whenever they please assume human shapes, and lie with women. Perhaps one of them appeared to this woman, and begot that young man of her.'

Chap. XIX—*Merlin's speech to the king's magicians, and advice about the building of the tower.*

Merlin in the meantime was attentive to all that had passed, and then approached the king, and said to him. 'For what reason am I and my mother introduced into your presence?' – 'My magicians,' answered Vortigern, 'advised me to seek out a man that had no father, with whose blood my building is to be sprinkled, in order to make it stand.' – 'Order your magicians,' said Merlin, 'to come before me, and I will convict them of a lie.' The king was surprised at his words, and presently ordered the magicians to come, and sit down before Merlin, who spoke to them after this manner: 'Because you are ignorant what it is that hinders the foundation of the tower, you have recommended the shedding of my blood for cement to it, as if that would presently make it stand. But tell me now, what is there under the foundation? For something there is that will not suffer it to stand.' The magicians at this began to be afraid, and made him no answer. Then said Merlin, who was also called Ambrose, 'I entreat your majesty would command your workmen to dig into the ground, and you will find a pond which causes the foundation to sink.' This accordingly was done, and presently they found a pond deep under ground, which had made it give way. Merlin after this went again to the magicians, and said, 'Tell me ye false sycophants, what is there under the pond.' But they were silent. Then said he again to the king, 'Command the pond to be drained, and at the bottom you will see two hollow stones, and in them two dragons asleep.' The king made no scruple of believing him, since he had found true what he said of the pond, and therefore ordered it to be drained: which done, he found as Merlin had said; and now was possessed with the greatest admiration of him. Nor were the rest that were present less amazed at his wisdom, thinking it to be no less than divine inspiration.

(Giles, 1896)

Accordingly, while Vortigern, King of the Britons was yet seated upon the bank of the pool that had been drained, forth issued the two dragons, whereof the one was white and the other red. And when the one had drawn anigh unto the other, they grappled together in baleful combat and breathed forth fire as they panted. But presently the white dragon did prevail, and drave the red dragon unto the verge of the lake. But he, grieving to be thus driven forth, fell fiercely again upon the white one, and forced him to draw back. And whilst that they were fighting on this wise, the King bade Ambrosius Merlin declare what this battle of the dragons did portend.

(Evans, 1912)

The symbolism of the Tower in the events immediately preceding Merlin's prophetic outburst demands some detailed examination. In the medieval period, this section of the *History* could have been understood as an allegory: false pride, evil and corruption, laid low. Today we are less inclined to give the allegory a moral or religious meaning, but a psychological interpretation which contains elements of both the ancient magical and the modern materialist maps of human consciousness.

The psychology of the nineteenth and twentieth century has tended to look to the east for traditional methods of analysing consciousness in support of its new techniques and theories. While this is not always the case (C.G. Jung's interest in both alchemy and astrology being good examples of adaptation of western traditional psychic topologies) it is a sad fact that many remarkable psychological expositions, either in the form of myth, allegory, or magical symbolism and methods, have been passed over in psychological research and publication. This omission is not entirely due to simple ignorance, but to the quite inaccurate claims that all wisdom teachings are essentially eastern.[1] When the wisdom of the east was rediscovered during the nineteenth century, it was applied as a corrective to the stultifying power of decayed Christianity, and considerable propaganda has accompanied this attitude right up to the present day, utterly ignoring many native traditions of expansion of consciousness.

The Tower of Vortigern may be interpreted upon several levels, and to come to grips with *The Prophecies*, we must first consider whether or not this allegory holds elements of an initiatory or catalytic system intended to transform individual consciousness.

It is significant that the description of the Tower and of Vortigern's treachery and weakness are intimately linked to Merlin, his mysterious birth, and the upsurge of prophetic vision. If the Tower was only a moralistic tale, we might dare to dismiss it as being a quaint description of evil getting its just deserts, but the connection to the act of prophecy, and the levels of symbolism leading to the rise of the Red and White Dragon, imply much more. There are also a number of Celtic folk tales which concern the subsidence of a building, or of a town, which may have coloured the sequence without necessarily being sources for it.[2]

As has been stated previously, Geoffrey of Monmouth drew heavily upon oral lore for his *History*. If we presume that the tale of the Tower is part of a widespread oral tradition, for there are Breton and Scottish examples of similar tales known even today, it is in keeping with the overall ambience of ancient lore that permeates the *History*.

In the larger sequence of events, the Tower is one of the most crucial scenes in Geoffrey's rambling narrative, and is so similar in imagery to certain magical and alchemical keys or processes, that we should interpret it as a 'wisdom tale', deriving from the remnants of oral teaching that persisted from pre-Christian belief and practice. There is evidence from the Mystery or esoteric systems concerning Tower, Pool, and paired Dragons; evidence that is both western and eastern, suggesting a worldwide tradition.[3]

The essential difference between the modern and ancient psychologies lies in their connection to two states of being: the land and the 'inner-planes'. Modern psychology is not concerned with either of these, but the transcendent systems of both west and east make much use of imaginative beings in other states or dimensions than those of everyday life, and of the importance of the natural environment as a psychic and spiritual unity in which humans play a central role.

We find these trans-personal themes in the story of the Tower; the eternal conflict between the Red and White Dragon is both historical and metaphysical – the environment linking

NORTH BAY
NORTH BAY
DEC 1982
PUBLIC LIBRARY

each together, or 'earthing' them through into generation and manifestation.

The construction of the Tower is also linked to a very primal theme, that of human sacrifice. We have an echo of the Celtic religion in this, for the early Celts were head-hunters, and were engaged in human sacrifice after it had been banned by the Roman Empire.[4] The extensive symbolism of Heads, Sacrifice, Natural sites and related myths and folk tales is an essential background to the theme reflected in the tale of Vortigern's Tower.[5]

Linked to this folkloric theme of sacrifice, is another startling attribute of Merlin: that he was born of a virgin (Nennius) or of the union of a maiden and an Otherworld being (Geoffrey). The two chroniclers reflect different variants of an extremely ancient theme: that of the special Child. It need hardly be added that this is found in orthodox Christianity, which revolves around a Virgin Birth and a Sacrifice. Is Merlin, therefore, being offered as a Christ-like being?[6]

Only the blood of a child born of a virgin can bind the mortar that holds the Tower together; a human sacrifice of a special being born under remarkable circumstances. It is this clearly defined background, derived from pagan rather than Christian symbolism, in which Merlin becomes a prophet. While the Tower is supposedly incomplete without the victim's blood, Merlin is not fully aware of his prophetic powers until he is confronted with the situation at the Tower. Merlin and the Tower, with its Pool, Stones or Vessels, and polarized Dragons, are intimately linked to one another. Like the constituents of an alchemical experiment (or of nuclear physics) they interact to produce an inevitable end result.

This picture of Merlin is rather different from that image accumulated by later accretions to the basic tales. He is young when he confronts Vortigern's false magicians at the Tower, he is presumably untrained, though his early training is referred to elsewhere by Geoffrey in enigmatic terms.[7] The deep master of wisdom is in fact an innocent youth, blessed or cursed with insight, whose very presence causes certain powers to come forth from the depths of the earth. These powers, the Dragons, cause the explosive Prophecies to be uttered. None of this, significantly, is concerned with religion, and certainly not with the orthodox Christianity of the Middle Ages. (*The Prophecies* were later placed on the *Index of Prohibited Books* by the Council of Trent in the sixteenth century, and remained prohibited until 1966 when Pope Paul VI cancelled the Index.)

During the twelfth century, there was sufficient fabulous and semi-pagan material in wide circulation, mainly oral, for many of the elements that outrage orthodoxy to be included in composite works such as the *History*. It is impossible for us to decide how intentional this pagan magical symbolism was on Geoffrey's part, but we can confirm from other authors such as Gerald du Barry that the pagan seership was active and not altogether prohibited. In 1172 a Welsh woman recounted a prophecy of Merlin to King Henry II that an English king, conqueror of Ireland, would die on a marvellous stone.[8]

The medieval popularity of the Sibylline Oracles,[9] plus a number of vernacular prophecies, is less likely to be a craze of the credulous period than a formalizing of widespread fragments previously known only in oral traditions, combined with classical or pseudo-classical texts.

When we say oral tradition, we must realize that such traditions were a central part of daily life in the medieval period, even as they are today in communities in some parts of Britain. While specific aspects of oral retention are evanescent, key themes are retained for many centuries. Geoffrey, therefore, is formalizing a body of knowledge or symbolism (by popular request and order of patronage, as he himself tells us) that would have been familiar to a large number of people, even if only in limited fragments, or fluid re-creations by travelling story-tellers.

It seems unavoidable, though utterly unproven, that this magical lore was inherited from the religion or teaching of the Druids. Setting aside any modern speculations, we have the evidence from classical historians and authors such as Julius Caesar that the Druids were an organized body that promulgated a system of wisdom held in respect by the ancient world. If the transformative symbolism relating to Merlin's inner awakening is not Druidic, it is nevertheless directly in keeping with certain well known themes found in mystical and magical initiations in both eastern and western systems of raising consciousness. Curiously, we often find oriental texts offered as evidence of the cultural age of meditative techniques (see for example *The Secret of the Golden Flower*, Jung and Wilhelm, Arkana, London 1984), yet similar symbolism in medieval works tends to be set aside.[10]

To establish the value of our text, Druidic or universal in its symbolism, we must first isolate the main elements. The categories that lead up to the Prophecies may be defined as follows: People, Places, Images, and Concepts.

These are the four primary elements of any Mystery, classical or native, in which a transpersonal wisdom or altered consciousness is taught through specific methods, and experienced by the individual through application of those methods.

By listing the components, and establishing the connections between them, we may define the magical initiatory or psychological content, and further compare this to similar material from a number of valuable sources with stated magical or metaphysical foundations.

PEOPLE:

Merlin: A youth, rumoured to be born without a father, of a royal mother, a maiden. His father is said to be an 'incubus daemon' (not related to the Christian orthodox concept of the evil 'demon'), a spirit dwelling 'between earth and the moon'.

Vortigern: A corrupt king, who has summoned destructive alien forces (the Saxons) to bolster up his rule. He has tried to retreat into a mountain fastness and build a tower, but fails.

The magicians: A group of false advisers who recommend human sacrifice. . . . They are, in fact, attempting to establish impossible conditions of repair for the Tower, and are maintaining their own best interests through confusion and obscurity.

Maugantius: An authority on incubi, probably one of the group of Magicians, or even introduced merely to explain Merlin's seeming virgin birth.

Merlin's Mother: a maiden of royal family, reputedly a virgin.

Dinabutius: Merlin's youthful companion.

PLACES

(A) Mount Erith. That Mount Erith is in fact Snowdon, has been proved by Tatlock.[11] It represents the 'Sacred Mountain' concept, as it appears in Welsh traditional lore.

(B) Kaermerdin: Merlin's home town. This is equated with the town of Carmarthen, and literally means 'Merlin's castle'.

(C) The Tower.

IMAGES

1 Merlin: image of young man of mysterious origin and paranormal powers. An innocent victim (in potential). Later to develop as source of prophetic insight and wisdom. *Image of spiritual potency*.

2 Vortigern: power-greedy and depraved king. *Image of uncontrolled lust*.

3 Magicians (and Maugantius): *Images of confusion and false knowledge* or deliberate misinformation and fraud.

4 Merlin's mother: *Image of virgin who conceives child of spirit*.

5 Mount Erith: a 'holy mountain'. *Image of initiatory place or state of higher consciousness*.

6 Kaermerdin: *Image of everyday collective world*.

7 Argument between Dinabutius and Merlin as to which is superior. This has strong recollection of a widespread folk theme, found elsewhere in the *History*, and in many myths, tales and ballads, of a magical conflict between two brothers. *Image of accusing and innocent brothers*.

8 The Tower. Built upon an inadequate foundation, as a refuge for the tyrannical usurping king. *Image of the false construct* (may be physical, psychic, or spiritual).

9 The Lake or Pool. Underneath the Tower, causing it to subside. *Image of the collective unconscious* (modern psychology) or *image of UnderWorld sea or pool of the Ancestors* (magical symbolism, not fully identical to the modern definition).

10 The Hollow Stones: Encysting the two Dragons. *Image of containing restrictive and protective vessels*.

11 The Red and White Dragons: opposing powers that fight until the end of Time in various manifestations which are

listed in the future-history encapsulated in the enigmatic Prophecies which follow. *Image of fundamental polarized energies* (may be physical, psychic, or spiritual).

12 The Dragon Flight and Prophecies: *Image of powers arising*; stimulating a mode of super-consciousness.

Within these twelve primary images, are a number of other images, which lead us into our last category of Concepts.[12]

CONCEPTS

1 The self-consuming nature of corruption. (Vortigern and Saxons)

2 The impossibility of building upon false foundations.

3 A sacrifice of innocence or spiritual power to reinforce (1) and (2).

4 A descent into levels that underpin the phenomena of the outer world (both physical and metaphysical).

5 A polarized power that rises out of the Earth or out of the depths of consciousness.

6 A new mode of consciousness that leaps across time and space.

Subsidiary images that link these sequences are:

1 The confrontation between Merlin and the false magicians, taking the form of a question and answer sequence that reveals progressive levels of the UnderWorld. (Beneath the Tower, the Lake; beneath the Lake, the Stones; within the Stones, the Dragons.)

2 The masons and workers draining the Lake. These are the functioning members of the King's retinue, or the operative modes of searching and working consciousness in pursuit of deeper levels.

3 King Vortigern sitting by the side of the drained Pool. An image of an individual at his lowest psychic ebb.

4 The image of Merlin bursting into tears. This is a particularly important relevant image, virtually a hallmark of the occurrence of genuine seership, to which we shall return below.

THE MEANING OF THE ALLEGORY OF THE TOWER

The assembly of royal and semi-royal persons, magicians, special buildings and natural forces is a recurring theme in esoteric symbolism, and a large number of parallel examples may be offered from various traditions. The close resemblance to alchemical symbolism is remarkable, and the entire passage of the confrontation and revelation leading to the arousal of the Dragon may be read as a typical alchemical text. As late as the seventeenth century, images similar to those employed in our example were being published as emblems and paradoxes in alchemical works.[13] It could be reasonably suggested that a certain amount of influence was exerted by the *History* and *The Prophecies* upon such works, yet no affirmed connection is made by the copious alchemical and metaphysical writers between their product and that of Geoffrey writing in the twelfth century.

Literary derivation plays an important part in the analysis of early texts, but in this instance we are discovering connections made within human consciousness at large, and reproduced in a multitude of examples sharing a common set of symbols and concepts.

Our analysis, therefore, combines elements from alchemy, magic, metaphysics and modern psychology, wherever they are found to connect in a harmonic manner. Having separated the building blocks of the edifice, the People, Places, Images, and Concepts, we may now reassemble them into a modern interpretation.

Vortigern represents the outer personality, particularly those conditioned and ruthless attitudes of dominance and survival of the false temporal 'self'. He is very much an unbalanced and incomplete figure, taking absurd steps to ensure a status of power that can only be, at best, limited by his own lifespan. He is an exaggerated allegory of the psychic state in which most of us live.

Moreover, Vortigern is a usurper, the rule that he tries to grasp is not his own, but truly belongs to another. This usurpation theme is common in expositions of both modern psychology and of ancient meditational techniques; a portion of the psyche steals the reins of power, and dominates the vast resources of consciousness that should be free and harmonized. According to traditional methods of attuning consciousness, we must remember the modern concept of the 'balanced personality' is still a usurping pseudo-entity. In the case of Vortigern, however, his imbalance is clearly stated.

The usurping King, who acts as a repulsive symbol of all that is destructive within ourselves, has drawn upon exterior agencies to bolster up his throne. Symbolized by 'the Saxons', the very forces that were foolishly invoked to gain power act as further corrosives. This represents the folly of attempting to strengthen oneself from outside, rather than from within.

The Magicians, who are clearly in contrast to Merlin, are the fallacious fragments of consciousness; delusions, false systems of knowledge; on a deeper level they epitomize the shadowy memories of ancient but outmoded and irrelevant practices. We might see them as filters or mediating aspects of the most accumulated detritus of imagination; in traditional symbolism they are the misleading beings who occupy the 'astral plane' and pretend to advise those foolish enough to listen to them in pursuit of power. They are, in fact, magical knowledge divorced from wisdom and the enlivening spirit; though their methods may work to a limited extent, the end product is weakness and imbalance.

It is significant that the false magicians suggest an ancient method of curing Vortigern's problem, and that their polarizing and challenging opposite, Merlin, refuses to take that potent but unnecessary path. The physical human sacrifice of an unwilling victim plays no part in true transformative magic.

The Tower is a well established symbol, with a long literary and historical currency. In our example it plays several roles, which are linked very closely together.

1   The Tower is a symbol of the state of consciousness represented by Vortigern. It is his structure of himself; a retreat from fear and cowardice, a false fortress built upon inadequate foundations. When this spurious edifice collapses, as it must, the King seeks advice from deluding sources rather than attempt to correct the weakness himself, or to be free to move his construct to another location.

2   In the broader context, we may regard the Tower as a

symbol of the psychic-body complexity, the apparently indissoluble set of connections that make up a human entity. It is, in effect, an outer expression of the King's inner state. The King in the Tower is the false personality that attempts to 'occupy' his or her own body, rather than attune to it upon a deeper and healthier level. The crumbling Tower is a state familiar to therapists, where psychic imbalance leads to physical illness.

This modern interpretation is built upon certain ancient key images, the best known being the Biblical 'Tower of Babel', and the Tarot Trump 'The Blasted Tower'. The Blasted Tower is not only a key that represents a human frailty or imbalance typical to us all, but operates on other levels that express the catalytic energies or breaking-down of any state or being or structure; even of the Universe itself. When a construct has remained intact or has been assembled through retentive fear and force, an external agency of catalysis will eventually destroy it.

This destruction, however, is the vital preliminary to fresh construction, on physical, psychic, or spiritual levels.

3   For Vortigern's Tower to be held together by the blood of a special child implies a magical act that was most abhorrent to any initiate who understood its implications. In this part of the tale, Geoffrey is recounting a very 'secret' theme, a method whereby time and change may be cheated by the application of perverted magic. Merlin's challenge to the false Magicians is similar to the challenges issued by other Prophets and visionaries, and to those of Jesus Christ.[14] He establishes a new pure state of consciousness (later to manifest in the outer form of the reign of Arthur) that supersedes the old corruption.

Merlin represents the eternal youth, the spiritual and enlivening consciousness; that innermost part of ourselves that is essential to truth and freedom. He is born of a virgin, or of a union between mortal and immortal; he is spirit made flesh. The parallel to Christ is unavoidable, but should not be understood in an orthodox religious sense. A practising Christian might say that Merlin was like Christ, but to a lesser degree. He is one of a number of special children, found in myth and religion from the earliest times, right up to the present day.

The King seeks to sacrifice the spiritual part of his life to maintain the temporal, ailing, edifice of his Tower. Merlin, however, *once summoned*, cannot be merely used or disposed of. The myth to which we referred above (the Two Brothers, Merlin and Dinabutius) gives us a clear image of the type frequently found in mystical allegories and meditational techniques that apply tuned specific visions. It is possible that Geoffrey or his story-telling source compressed the broadly disseminated Celtic folk tale of two comrades or brothers fighting for the love of a girl into our present sequence. They represent the powers of giving and taking, under the Goddess.

We may use this imagery as follows: the King's messengers are seeking a youth born without a father. At the gates of a town, called Kaermerdin two youths are overheard in conflict. One accuses the other of being born without a father, thus alerting the King's men. Following the mythical course of the Two Brothers, or the Accuser and the Innocent, this scene represents everyday consciousness and the outer world, at the gates of which are two beings or poles of awareness. In the old tales these are Cain and Abel, Horus and Set, Beli and Bran, Jack and John. (Although the folk and mythical theme is not overtly stated by Geoffrey, he employs it elsewhere in the *History*.)[15]

This is actually our first contact with the theme of Polarity, which is repeated in subsequent and more powerful encounters: Vortigern and Merlin's mother; the confrontation between Merlin and the Magicians; and the battle between the Two Dragons.

From collective consciousness, therefore, the King's men bring Merlin the Innocent, and his Mother the Maiden. Before dealing directly with Merlin himself, the King must first discover the nature of Merlin's conception, by learning it from his mother.

We may see a further implication in this order of events that the tale is an echo, distant but clear, of an older myth. There is something supernatural about Merlin's birth, and something sacred about his virgin mother. She is a reflection of a Celtic goddess, or of the mysterious virgins who conceive known in pagan religious myth and practice. Esoterically, she epitomizes the mediating and enabling Female Power; she is an expression of the Great Mother who gives birth to the Son of Light.

Before the King can speak directly to the mysterious Child, he has to understand the nature of the magical Birth; this can only be gained by converse with the Mother.

That such a mystical theme should be embodied in a slightly scurrilous tale, common in many variants in the Middle Ages,[16] is typical of the Mysteries. At its most extreme we find this theme in Alchemy where the Stone of the Philosophers is said to be in common dirt, or in magical gnosis, where the pure virgin is also a whore.

On a less exalted level, but no less important, there is a psychological value and method, one which is applied in meditational and therapeutic techniques. If we consider an essential ingredient missing from the unbalanced Vortigern, who is willing to summon up spiritual or innocent energies for selfish sacrifice, we come to the obvious conclusion that he is sexually imbalanced; he lacks the female element. He is the stereotype of the aggressive grasping male, using the most ridiculous means to gain trivial ends for himself. When his messengers (or questing mental signals, shown in traditional magic by certain orders of innerworld beings) find the youth Merlin, his Mother must come also, as she is his primal origin.

In Vortigern's conversation with the Mother, we may read a simple communication with inner female qualities, a vital element in meditation, mental therapy, and magical initiation. The learned disquisition of Maugantius, in which Apuleius is (wrongly) cited, gives us an amusing clue as to how the Female power should *not* be regarded – for she is much more than a means to an end. This failure on Vortigern's part to understand anything that happens to him as a result of the Merlin experience is a constant to which we shall return later.[17]

The confrontation

Merlin now challenges Vortigern, who admits to the advice of his magicians, that a fatherless man must be sacrificed to enable the Tower to stand.

This is one of the curious quirks that are typical of traditional tales and ballads: there is no common-sense reason why Vortigern must admit at this stage that he has a murderous motive, unless we assume that he is confident of having Merlin in his power. Many such leaps of sense in traditional lore imply a magical or mythical sequence, usually connected to the inevitable nature of certain revelations or confessions.[18]

Following our magical/psychological exposition, the King's confession comes immediately after his conversation with Merlin's mother, and upon a direct challenge from the young Merlin himself. Vortigern cannot deny the truth of his actions when challenged. He is compelled to reveal his secret plan or desire; and no individual can hide the truth from his or her innermost consciousness, no matter how separated these inner and outer natures seem to have become.

The allegory is one of disparate levels or entities within one individual consciousness; of primal magical energies relating to the land and the people within it epitomized through the agency of the Crown; and of specific magical and meditational techniques and maps of the innerworld which may be applied both individually and collectively. It is on the individual level, as a means of altering awareness, or of gaining a deeper understanding of one's true self, that the Merlin sequence is of value to the modern mind.

Having challenged Vortigern, Merlin now challenges the false magicians. So potent is his challenge, that they are struck dumb, and can give him no answer, a Celtic theme that is found in the tale of the bard Taliesin, another 'Christ-like' figure.[19]

We now begin the most technical and important part of the sequence, a descent into the UnderWorld. As shown in Figure 3, the entire scene is a stratified psychic or magical key.

1   In a surrounding landscape, we see the invading Saxons on one hand, and the peaceful community (Caermerdin) on the other. This idealized stereotypical image is of the sort used in meditative visualization, and is extremely ancient in origin. Before proceeding further with our description, it may also be observed that the accumulated imagery is very reminiscent of a psychopompic sequence; we may be

TOWER OF VORTIGERN

examining not only a magical drama in which initiation is conferred, but also a visionary map for the departed soul.[20]

2   In the middle of our idealized picture, in the distance, is a mountain (Mount Erith) on which a Tower stands in a state of collapse or ruin.

3   Beneath the Tower is the first hidden realm, the Lake or Pool. In our idealized picture, we can see into the Mountain – a device commonly used in Alchemical illustrations.

4   At the bottom of the Pool is the second hidden level, two Stones or Vessels. We are able to see inside these Stones.

5   Within the Stones are the Red and White Dragons.[21]

Merlin's challenge to the magicians, in the form of unanswered questions, proceeds through each level. We are descending into the UnderWorld, a descent beloved of Celtic folklore and myth, and one which must have been widespread in old tales and songs in Geoffrey's Brittany and Wales.[22]

The King causes the Pool to be drained, and the truth of Merlin's revelation is known.

The arousal of the Dragons

After the descent through Three Worlds or levels of consciousness, we find King Vortigern sitting by the side of the drained pool. This image is similar to those employed in later alchemical texts, where a King or old man is sitting (under a Saturnine influence) looking miserable, awaiting the advent of the Black Crow. This is the lowest psychic ebb, the draining of psychic reactions which leaves the individual utterly blank and unpolarized. It is the prelude to an even more shattering experience in the magical psychology, and means far more than mere 'depression'. In mystical works this stage is sometimes called 'the dark night of the soul'.

Two further levels are known in the magical system, levels which are not included in modern psychology. These are shown by the Stones and the Dragons.

Before dealing with the arousal of the Dragons, we should summarize the events leading up to it.

1   The unbalanced King seeks to build an impossible Tower.
2   He summons a sacrificial victim, a pure youth, to consecrate the work with his blood.
3   The pure youth reveals mysteries that lie beneath the Tower, and the King orders work that reveals these mysteries, even though he is not fully aware of the implications of this act.
4   The youth, Merlin, and the King, Vortigern, are both present at the edge of the drained Pool when the Dragons emerge.

As suggested above, this fourfold sequence may operate within individual consciousness through meditation and visualization. It is the presence of the King and the Youth at the Drained Pool that enables the Dragons to burst forth from their containing Vessels or Stones.

The student of westernized texts on Yoga will recognize that this progression is almost identical to that of the methods of Tantra or the scientific art of Kundalini yoga.[23] This 'secret' power system, known in the west as the Arousal of the Inner Fire, lies at the core of all mystical, meditative and magical practices.

The false assumption that such methods were unknown in the west until imported from the east in the nineteenth century is now virtually exploded, and the Merlin text alone is ample proof that symbolism of this type was known during the medieval period, even if we do not cite any of the classical or ecclesiastical sources that reveal an intimate knowledge of this type of inner operation.

As the 'Inner Fire' is one of the fundamental properties of polarized life energies, some instruction or understanding of its arousal plays a central part in all schools of psychology, be they religious, magical, or materialist. While the emphasis and the language changes, the Inner Fire remains.

The sexual element is explicit in the story of Merlin's virgin mother, who may or may not have consorted with an Otherworld being. In terms of the individual psyche, it is the summoning of the female power (symbolized in western magic by goddess images) that awakens Merlin, the blessed youth, and so causes the King to drain the pool of 'unconsciousness' or Ancestral images.

The two Stones are vessels that encyst the Dragons. As in Alchemy, they must be shattered or dissolved, to liberate the power enclosed within.

In our example it is the interaction between the King, the Mother, and the Child, that causes these encysted energies to be liberated. Once freed, they are found to be a Red and White Dragon, the most primal embodiments of positive and negative polarity. In magical techniques, these energies lie quiescent at the base of the spine (i.e. below the Tower) until aroused by meditation, or more unusually, by magical ritual. A great deal of training is given in learning how to prepare for this uprush, the Inner Fire, and to direct it to the seat of apparent consciousness in the Head.

This is exactly what happens with Merlin, for once the Dragons are aroused and begin to fight (interact), he is propelled by one question from the King: 'what does it mean?' into a full prophetic trance.[24]

The energies aroused have stimulated consciousness into a new and accelerated mode, one in which time, space, and the land coalesce into a flow of images and potent symbols.

At this point in the narrative, Geoffrey advises us that 'Merlin immediately burst into tears'. This is a very genuine description of a physical reaction known to seers, meditators and even to psychotherapists. It does not necessarily imply grief, but is an inevitable physical reaction to the stimulus of some strong inner impulse. Meditators and practitioners of magic will confirm that their eyes weep when their inner being makes some contact with a state or dimension beyond the normal comprehension, and that this occurs during states in which personal or trivial emotion is superseded or suspended.

The nature of the prophetic power

Before returning to the allegory, and to Vortigern's reaction to the Prophecies, the appearance of the Dragons is an appropriate point to discuss other references in the *History* to Merlin's prophetic power. As detailed analysis of the magical or metaphysical lore is given in other chapters, this section is brief, merely showing where Geoffrey or his source from oral tradition has added to the picture of the prophetic experience which we are examining.

1   *Merlin is not a magician* Contrary to popular belief, the Merlin of *The Prophecies*, and of the *History* at large, is not a waver of wands and maker of incantations.[25] It is very clear that he is of a different order altogether, and this is further emphasized by his confrontation with the magicians of Vortigern. He does not achieve his prophecies by spells, invocation, or even astrology, though, as we shall see, they do contain some significant astrological material.

2   *Merlin cannot prophesy idly* When Aurelius asks Merlin for a prevision regarding a great monument (later to become Stonehenge) he replies 'Mysteries of this kind are not to be revealed but when there is greatest necessity for it. If I should pretend to utter them for ostentation or for diversion, the spirit that instructs me would be silent, and would leave me when I should have occasion for it.' We may take this as referring to instruction from a source in the Otherworld (which is Tatlock's opinion), but as the character of Merlin is defined by the story of his special birth and his spiritual qualities, it seems more likely to relate to that spiritual source of inspiration: 'drawing the breath of prophecy, he burst into tears and spake . . . '. This same spiritual power (quite distinct from a familiar spirit or daemon, which is a being and not a state of being) has well known religious parallels.[26]

3   *Merlin can interpret* He reveals the meaning of 'a star of great magnitude and brilliance' that heralds a new age (VIII,15), and this is a stellar event seen by people throughout the land. He applies his powers of interpretation to the Prophecies, and as we have discussed elsewhere, is able to withdraw from the high flights of seership into regular far-seeing or prediction of immediate events. It is at this point that we may return to the allegory of Vortigern and the Tower, which re-opens with the main narrative of the *History*, after the prophetic verses have ceased.

CHAPTER 6
The eternal questions

Merlin, by delivering these and many other prophecies caused in all that were present an admiration at the ambiguity of his expressions. But Vortigern above all the rest both admired and applauded the wisdom and prophetical spirits of the young man: for that age had produced none that ever talked in such a manner before him. Being therefore curious to learn his own fate, he desired the young man to tell him what he knew concerning that particular. Merlin answered: – 'Fly the fire of the sons of Constantine, if you are able to do it: already are they fitting out their ships: already are they leaving the Armorican shore: already are they spreading out their sails to the wind. They will steer towards Britain: they will invade the Saxon nation: they will subdue that wicked people; but they will first burn you being shut up in a tower. To your own ruin did you prove a traitor to their father, and invite the Saxons into the island. You invited them for your safeguard; but they came for a punishment to you. Two deaths instantly threaten you; nor is it easy to determine, which you can best avoid. For on the one hand the Saxons shall lay waste your country, and endeavour to kill you: on the other shall arrive the two brothers, Aurelius Ambrosius and Uther Pendragon, whose business will be to revenge their father's murder upon you. Seek out some refuge if you can: to-morrow they will be on the shore of Totness. The faces of the Saxons shall look red with blood, Hengist shall be killed, and Aurelius Ambrosius shall be crowned. He shall bring peace to the nation: he shall restore the churches; but shall die of poison. His brother Uther Pendragon shall succeed him, whose days also shall be

65

cut short by poison. There shall be present at the commission of this treason your own issue, whom the boar of Cornwall shall devour.' Accordingly the next day early, arrived Aurelius Ambrosius and his brother, with ten thousand men.

(Giles, 1896)

Vortigern, the model of unbalanced selfishness, hears the future history of the land of Britain, the ending of the world, and then asks only about his own fate.

If we follow our use of Vortigern as an allegorical persona, it is clear that he misses the true value of *The Prophecies* altogether. Like any one of us who seeks supernatural guidance for selfish ends, he hears only bad news; Ambrosius Aurelius and his brother are about to land and destroy him. Nevertheless, Vortigern has at least asked for elucidation of part of the future, and Merlin exhibits some of the properties of his foresight. This response to Vortigern's question about his own fate is not prophecy, but a combination of far-seeing and common-sense. Although Geoffrey of Monmouth has written this scene, rather than draw it almost verbatim from oral sources, he still holds to the pattern of the prophetic insight, and its lesser harmonic of simple prediction.

The interplay between Vortigern, Merlin, and the remarkable imagery of *The Prophecies*, is reminiscent of another sequence of wonders that appeared in medieval literature not long after Geoffrey's *History* was circulated. There is little doubt that the Merlin lore in *The History* is connected to the Mystery of the Grail, in which a revelation occurs, and the candidate must be able to *ask the correct question* to enter into the heart of the Mystery itself.

The pattern suggested by the allegory of Vortigern and Merlin, with the prophetic sequence from tradition, should be considered as a forerunner of the later refined and more Christian Grail lore. In the case of Vortigern, he fails the test; he cannot understand the nature of inner revelation, he expects magic to work independently of spiritual reality, and when presented with a sequence of wonders that reaches right to the end of time, he can only think to ask about his own miserable fate.

When Merlin, in later developments of the Arthurian theme,

initiates the search for the Grail, he seeks to open out a further cycle of revelation; repairing that which Vortigern destroyed, revealing that which Vortigern confused.

It is significant that Arthur's realm is traditionally destroyed by fruit of incest (Mordred), for this theme is first discovered in connection with Vortigern. While hiding in his Tower (soon to be burned by Aurelius Ambrosius) Vortigern attempts to father children upon his daughter in a vain attempt to perpetuate his line. The Tower, which began the allegory, is to be Vortigern's doom. Trapped by the avenging Ambrosius, the usurping King is burned within his Tower. Having failed to understand the nature of the inner powers of life, the inflated personality is destroyed by agencies from outside himself. In the simplest sense, this is the death that comes to us all; but it also demonstrates a major law of metaphysics or magic. If we are unable to maintain an inner balance, the correcting energy *appears* to come from without.

This law is often confused with the popular notion of 'karma', derived from a misunderstanding of eastern philosophy. In western esoteric models, the law is usually demonstrated upon the Tree of Life glyph, in which the entire structure is held in balance by a sequence of polarizations. Vortigern is actually an empty shell; his spirit has been withdrawn, leaving an inner vacuum. The avenging powers, dramatized in the *History* as Aurelius and Uther, are shown in medieval magic as 'fiery angels', the Seraphim of Biblical tradition who bear flaming swords.

The Tarot image of the Blasted Tower shows the destruction of a tower by lightning, the traditional agency of divine retribution. A man and a woman fall from the Tower: in our allegory they are Vortigern and his daughter. While there is no proof that Geoffrey saw a formalized image such as the Tarot card, or that the picture employed in the card is derived from Geoffrey's tale, there can be no doubt that both are grounded in the same symbolic foundation.

The theme of evil and retribution makes stirring tales, but the subtle implication of the tale of Vortigern leads us to the magical and spiritual laws of inner development. Vortigern's failure to connect to his innermost self, his reality, causes the energies of that reality to approach him outwardly; not through any motive of vengeance (though this may be the superficial expression) but through an ultimate law of balance and harmony. That which is broken down is then rebuilt.

Merlin is the agency of king-making and king-breaking, both for Vortigern and for Arthur. If, for example, Vortigern had succeeded in his sacrifice of the youthful Merlin, he would have temporarily buttressed his Tower. If he had understood the revelation of *The Prophecies*, or had asked the *correct question* after the future of the land had been uttered, he might have been able to adjust his kingship into a better state. Vortigern, however, was too far into his own corrupted self-image, and could only be purified by fire.

Merlin then proceeds to aid the rightful royal house, and to disguise Uther and aid him in his love for Igerna or Ygraine. The mysterious child that is created is Arthur, who represents a second cycle of the problems and solutions attempted by Vortigern. We may see in the conception of Arthur an echo of the supernatural conception of Merlin; both occur in a situation where a woman does not know the true nature of her lover, both are matters of a high destiny linked to the land of Britain.

Before moving on to the meaning of *The Prophecies* themselves, and their rather remarkable accuracy of prediction in some cases, we should not neglect that Question, left unasked by Vortigern.

THE QUESTION

In the Grail legends, it is a Question that frees the Fisher King from his infirmity, and restores the Waste Land to fruitfulness. Sometimes the Question is 'What does it mean?' implying a further revelation of the mystical Procession of the Grail implements; this is a compression of a question and answer sequence in which the identity of the Grail, the King, and the Land are fully unified. Such sequences are found in a number of tales and ballads, and often involve riddles or exchanges of questions that counteract one another. The system is very ancient indeed, and rooted in the sources of polarized consciousness that we share with each other, with our ancestors, and in relationship to the Land or World.

Vortigern managed to ask 'What does it mean', but turned this into 'What does it mean for me?', and so sealed his inevitable doom. Throughout this book, we are considering answers to that first part of the Question – 'What does it mean?', and the conclusion drawn from the various strands of meaning is this:

We can experience dramatically altered states of perception in which time, space and interaction are suspended. The second part of the Question, therefore, may be 'How do I experience this for myself?' Like all such mystical or magical questions, the pattern is threefold, and a third questioning element is the most significant and superficially absurd.

1 *'What does it mean?'* What is the meaning of life itself? (shown by the struggle of the Red and White Dragon) The answer is an enigmatic set of prophecies, containing methods of altering awareness, predictions of the future, and an apocalyptic vision of the ending of the Solar System. In other words, the meaning cannot be communicated intellectually, it has to work through an analogous process within the individual; a stream of symbols and images rather than a mere explanation.

2 *'How do I experience this for myself?'* The individual seeks to enter into that state of consciousness experienced by the ancient seers and prophets, to gain firsthand knowledge of the higher harmonics of reality that are hinted at in the poetical images and paradoxical verses.

The methods are already present in the Prophecies themselves, and must be worked within the individual psyche. As we shall see in our following chapters, the text contains a number of key images for visualization, meditation, or even magical invocation. These are the means whereby a direct experience may be gained.

3 *'What happens next?'* Only a true poet would dare to ask this question – not as an intellectual query, but as a fresh model of perception, a new realm of consciousness extending beyond the catalysis and destruction shown in the last few verses of *The Prophecies*. No mere book can supply an answer to this type of magical or spiritual question – only

our own experience and inward cognition can tell us what lies beyond the limits of created patterns of existence.

In our remaining chapters, we shall progress through *The Prophecies* to their awesome conclusion.

PART II

The power in practice

Prediction, invocation, and apocalyptic
vision through the traditional
British Prophecies

CHAPTER 7

The interpretation of The Prophecies, *sixth to twenty-first centuries AD*

The main text employed in the interpretation is the translation published by Giles in *Six Old English Chronicles*, where the entire *History* is translated. A few lines have been clarified by application to other translations or to the Latin or through inspiration, but the Giles translation is followed closely in most cases.[1]

Much of the original text seems to be in a threefold pattern, and this can be clearly found in the sense and progression of the translated material. Geoffrey's Latin verse confirms this poetical theme, and the Welsh Druid sayings are frequently couched in Triadic form. The numbered examples in our text are generally triads, though in some cases there are single lines. The single lines are often sequences of importance, or of compressed time passage, but some of the lines are merely misplaced.

There is no attempt or pretence at re-ordering or clarification of the text or its translation in a scholarly manner; the scholarship on the language has been done by experts, and is referred to or discussed elsewhere. The numbering of each section or triad is merely for convenience, and does not refer to any numbering in the Latin or in translated texts. This presentation of *The Prophecies*, therefore, is for the benefit of ease of reading; the text is separated into units that were perhaps triadic verses in the lost Welsh original, but in any case make sense. The commentary follows each verse.

The commentary and analysis is divided into two general aspects, historical and mythological. In many cases these categories overlap, and the historical notes are often based upon traditional history, particularly in the earliest episodes. The mythic material is discussed wherever obviously symbolic themes arise, but also refers to a possible sub-text, or magical and psychological method that seems to permeate some of the scenes described. In many cases, this aspect simply is not present, and so is not included in the commentary.

The historical material eventually becomes inaccessible, as it seems to extend beyond our present period, and at this stage the Mythical commentary prevails. In the last part of *The Prophecies*, we are entirely in the realm of vision, stellar imagery, and recondite themes of cosmic evolution. Some of these are discussed in the opening chapters, while others are dealt with as they arise in the Merlin text.

The historical correlation is necessarily brief, partly because this correlation is of less importance than the magical and psychological implications of *The Prophecies*, and partly because it would be pointless to recapitulate episodes of British history which are well known or dealt with in detailed books already. King Alfred, for example, is given his place on the timescale of *The Prophecies*; there is no need to deal with the achievements of his reign in detail, as he can be found in any good history book. Wherever possible the early dates listed are the most recently agreed in historical publication; if in doubt they are given as approximate dates.

In some of the more difficult and obscure verses, an interpretation seems impossible. Such cases are merely given and left to the reader to judge or discard. Many of the difficult examples have imagery or themes that may be commented upon sensibly without attempting an interpretation; fabulous beasts are a commonplace visionary motif, for example, and these are discussed even when it is not clear if they have any historical cross-reference.

Interpretation of prophetic verses is not, or should not be, a demonstration of an author's intellectual deviousness and agility. Most of the correlations offered are very obvious, have been found by earlier commentators, and should be clear to the reader. They also follow a time scale, and once a few obvious anchoring points have been established, most of the rest is common sense, as far as the historical aspects are concerned.

The magical, symbolic, psychological, and visionary elements are a different matter, and more deserving of attention. While no attempt has been made to contrive a historical correspondence for every single line, word and image in *The Porphecies*, the metaphysical elements are given as much attention as possible in a book of limited size.

The Prophecies reveal an active and applicable system of transpersonal psychology, although it is couched in confused language and a mixture of Classical and British imagery. They also contain a mystical vision of reality and consciousness which has ancient precedents, and which is an experience that may be attained by anyone applying his or her self to the traditional methods of altering awareness, many of which are shown in the imagery itself.

Furthermore, *The Prophecies* are the earliest text which demonstrates some of the political/visionary traits that permeated British culture up to the time of the Second World War, occurring in cycles, and perhaps beginning to arise afresh today.

Finally, the interpretations offered are intended to stimulate fresh insights into the nature of Merlin himself. Historical 'proof' and 'factual evidence' are more easily fabricated than smoke-rings, but a constant theme and a firm powerful inner nature and identity are less easy to fake. Merlin, as first described by Geoffrey, is very well defined, and these prophetic verses reveal the methods, the insights, and ultimately the fate, of Merlin and of his heirs.

Who then *are* the heirs of Merlin? In one sense we all inherit his influence through time; in historical and cultural patterns epitomized by the models of Arthur's court which he helped to create, in ethical terms by his refusal to be a sacrifice to dark powers, and in magical terms through the specifically western and British meta-psychology associated with his name. It is this last area in which his direct heirs and pupils are found, for those who apply to this system of defining and altering consciousness are literally under the tutelage of Merlin. Other figures stand out in the inner vision as heirs and teachers, but Merlin stands at the head of the fountain, and awaits our questioning awareness.

THE HISTORICAL CORRELATIONS:
A NOTE OF WARNING

The following set of correlations are not offered as the true and only meaning of *The Prophecies of Merlin*; they are merely one possible chronological interpretation, seen through the eyes of the twentieth century. The medieval commentator Alanus de Insulis shrewdly observed that each generation would make its own expansion of *The Prophecies*; poetically this is a property of the prophetic insight, which expands with each expansion of human progress and consciousness. More prosaically, we are all free to add whatever correlations time and events have thrown up for us upon the tide of the centuries.

I would like to forestall, at the outset, the flood of objections and disproving letters, comments, or articles that any such correlation will inevitably arouse. I do not uphold that the historical examples are the correct or exact correlations, and I am only too happy to hear of alternatives. There are more than sufficient remarkable psychological insights and startling previsions in the Merlin text; we need not waste time quibbling over historical details or time scales.

Because my attitude is not one of factual 'proof' mongering, there is no attempt to cross refer the following analysis to a number of commentaries from the thirteenth to the nineteenth century; each commentator has applied his own time scale and intuitions or beliefs; some are wildly mystical, others are literary. I would encourage the reader to use his or her own imagination to bring *The Prophecies of Merlin* alive, and to be aware that no matter how the historical material is correlated, there will always be someone who disagrees, or who seeks the petty challenge of 'disapproving' that which belongs in realms where proof is less valid than imagination or intuition.

Having stated my case, I must add that any historical inaccuracies, omissions, or misrepresentations of hard fact are, of course, my sole responsibility.

COMMENTARY ON *THE PROPHECIES*

1   *Woe to the Red Dragon, for his banishment hasteneth on. His lurking holes shall be seized by the White Dragon, which signifies the Saxons whom you invited over; but the Red denotes the British nation, which shall be oppressed by the White. Therefore shall its mountains be levelled as the valleys, and the rivers of the valleys shall run with blood.*

During the first part of *The Prophecies*, that leading up to events in Geoffrey's own period, we are dealing with events which were known to the chronicler, the translator, or to the bard who might repeat the traditional verses upon which Geoffrey's Latin text is based. Although there is a certain proportion of the overall text that jumps forward or backward from a progressive chronological sequence, we can apply plenty of hindsight to these early, confirmed, verses, as surely Geoffrey must have done. Some of this part of *The Prophecies* seems to be drawn from Nennius (*Historia Britonum*, ninth century), but regardless of the obvious conclusion that it all could have been assembled from hindsight, there are sub-textual elements and a moral and metaphysical theme which is developed throughout the remainder of the text, leading up to the cosmic and apocalyptic vision in the final verses.

HISTORICALLY this refers to Vortigern's famous invitation to the Saxons, to act as mercenaries and help in the battle against invading Irish and Picts (approximately AD 450). As both traditional and modern history advise us, the Saxons merely increased their hold upon the land during this period, holding the British to ransom. Despite attempts to resist the Saxons, the newcomers made persistent claims upon territory. After the death of his son Vortimer, and the massacre of three hundred British elders during a peace conference, Vortigern fled to the fastnesses of Wales, building a retreat on Mount Snowdon.

MYTHICALLY we may recognize certain symbolic elements mingled with the factual material. Prior to the first prophetic utterance from Merlin, we have discovered Vortigern, a traitorous king, attempting to build a Tower for defence against the very forces that he had invoked for his own aid and benefit. (See Chapter 5, 'Vortigern's Tower' for a full analysis.)

There are parallels in alchemy, folklore, and orthodox religious themes, to the sequence of imagery and historical events that lead up to the discovery of Merlin and his utterances.

The historical relationship between Vortigern and the Saxons has become attached to a magical or psychological theme. Vortigern's Tower falls because it is built upon a false foundation; and beneath this foundation again are warring energies. These are historically expressed as the Britons and Saxons, but are inwardly the energies of the individual psychic-biological matrix. There is a further correlation between the Dragons and the energies of the Land itself, earth energies which seem to have occupied the time and attention of the ancients considerably. Although this is a pre-historic theme, dating from the times when massive stone and earth structures were erected and aligned, we find it connected to the character of Merlin, to the symbol of the Dragon, and to the quality or magical nature of Kingship.[2]

The King digs down into the roots of the Land (the depths of the UnderWorld of consciousness and of metaphysics) and the Dragons found therein are awakened.

Merlin is transformed, from a victim to an active power of far-seeing consciousness. His latent seership is triggered by the primal energies of the Red and White Dragons; in the consciousness of the King, he is the source of knowledge of normally forbidden or inaccessible realms. He utters not only the immediate future, but the entire gamut of events through to the end of time.

Vortigern, however, misunderstands the value of this utter-ance or mode of consciousness, and his response is to ask after the manner of his own death – he fails the moment of enlightenment.

This failure of Vortigern is made very clear not only by the historical defeat that he undergoes, but by other legendary elements attached to his personal fate. His son dies, his elders are massacred, he retreats to a Tower (built after the Dragons have gone forth), where he encourages Merlin to charm his days away with hallucinations. He even attempts incest with his daughter, to regenerate his line.[3]

The individual, magical, social and historical themes are closely interwoven, but the die is cast, and Vortigern's failure sets the scene for a second cycle, that of the line of Arthur.[4]

2   *The exercise of religion shall be destroyed, and churches be laid open to ruin. At last the oppressed shall prevail, and oppose the cruelty of foreigners. For a Boar of Cornwall shall give his assistance, and trample their necks under his feet.*

HISTORICALLY This represented to Geoffrey and his contemporaries the arrival from Brittany of the line of Arthur: Aurelius and Uther (Pendragon), the sons of Constantine. Under Arthur, son of Uther, the invaders were conquered and a period of strength and peace was achieved. Exactly how accurate this may be in terms of factual history is uncertain, and still the subject of much debate.

The destruction of religion relates to the Saxon disruption of the Christian churches, established under the old Celtic Church. It is also a theme which recurs in *The Prophecies* in a more symbolic or ethical and visionary sense, and we will return to it several times in the course of our analysis.

Traditionally Arthur, product of the Boar of Cornwall, defeated the Saxons at Mount Badon, in the early years of the sixth century.

MYTHICALLY Apart from the first introduction of the recurring theme of the ruin of orthodox religion, there is no deeper meaning to these lines, as we have emerged from a magical flow of symbolism into a stretch of basic historical statement of events.

3   *The islands of the ocean shall be subject to his power, and he shall possess the forests of Gaul. The house of Romulus shall dread his courage, and his end shall be doubtful. He shall be celebrated in the mouths of the people, and his exploits shall be as meat and drink to those who relate them.*

HISTORICALLY AND MYTHICALLY there is little separation between the inner and outer elements of this triad. The semi-historical Arthur was crowned as King of Britain, and he made expeditions into Europe (i.e. Gaul). In Welsh tales, he conquered even the remnants of the failing Roman Empire, the last of the house of Romulus. This is all potential hindsight, with Geoffrey reinforcing in *The Prophecies* the themes that are written into the broader tapestry of *The History*. We shall find this miniature mirroring again, and it is almost tempting to consider that Geoffrey's famous and lost 'British Book' was in fact *The Prophecies*, which he expanded and compounded with other chronicles, histories, and a collection of traditional themes from Welsh lore, classical allusion, and orthodox religious interpretation.[5]

The reference to the end of the Boar being doubtful is an allusion to the theme that Arthur did not die, but was carried to Avalon where he awaits the time of his return to save the Britons. Geoffrey later says that Arthur was taken to the 'INSULA AVALLONIS' (1X,4,X1,2) after his battle with Mordredus. In this island the sword Caliburn was forged. A Welsh saying reminds us that it is 'not wise' to suggest that Arthur has a grave!

In the last line, we are reminded of the oral and traditional currency of the Arthurian theme. To merit such a statement from Geoffrey, the Arthurian lore must have been widespread during his own time, and once again he deliberately draws our attention to the fact that his material is drawn from the native (Celtic) oral histories. This is a faint forerunner, too, of the political and Pan-Celtic mood that sometimes creeps into the Prophecies, for Arthur was the emblem of the rising of the Celts into freedom and unity against foreign oppression. The conflict between Saxons and Britons is perhaps being used suggestively to imply the conflict between the native British or Welsh and the Norman invading aristocracy of Geoffrey's day.[6]

We might add that here is our first predictive element, for after Geoffrey's development of the traditional Arthurian theme, it blossomed into literary acceptance during the twelfth century, and continued to develop with each succeeding century to the present day. Perhaps Geoffrey himself might be surprised if he could see just how extensively Arthur is extolled in the prose, poems, music, songs, plays and films known to us today, eight centuries after he first set down the British oral traditions into manuscript.

4 *Six of his posterity shall sway the sceptre, but after them shall arise a German Worm. This worm shall be exalted by a Seawolf, whom the woods of Africa shall accompany.*

HISTORICALLY This refers to the semi-legendary history of the post-Arthurian period, in which the Kingdom collapsed under local strife and further invasions. Gildas names five tyrants who are not historically proven: Constantine, Caninus, Vortipor, Cuneglasus, and Maglocunus. These are fairly British or Celtic names in character, Maglocunus being a god-name from the Romano-British period.[7] In the middle of the sixth century, a Saxon invasion made considerable inroads into the south of England. The West Saxons defeated the British at Dyrham (577), and occupied Bath, Gloucester, and Cirencester. It is to this period that the emigrations to Brittany are traditionally ascribed, in which a Celtic/British connection established from pre-Roman times was reinforced by people fleeing the Saxons. Culturally, we now know that contact and regular exchange between Greater and Lesser Britain (England and Wales and Brittany) was in fact constant and well developed over several centuries.

MYTHICALLY Curiously, just as the Sons of Constantine, the line that represented the true British throne, arrived from Brittany to defeat the usurper Vortigern, so did a later line of kings (the Stuarts) have a seemingly 'Breton' origin. The same poetical and mystical doom was attached to the Stuarts in a much later historical cycle as that which affected Arthur – they were the first kings of a united Britain (with James VI and I), and after the Revolution, were both political and poetical 'Kings over the Water'.

The Stuart-Hanoverian conflict, now apparently long resolved, is yet another cycle of the battle of the Red and White Dragons, the 'British' and the 'Germans'. Merlin returns to this theme frequently, and with some accuracy.

> 5   *Religion shall again be abolished, and there shall be a*
> *movement of the metropolitan Sees./The dignity of London*
> *shall adorn Dobernia, and the seventh pastor of York shall*
> *be visited in the kingdom of Armorica./Menevia shall put on*
> *the pall of the City of Legions, and a Preacher of Ireland*
> *shall be dumb on account of an infant growing in the womb.*

HISTORICALLY This refers directly to the increased emigration to Brittany in the middle of the sixth century, and the Celtic or British Church (presumably restored during the reign of Arthur) was affected, particularly by movement of bishops to Brittany. Menevia, St David's, is moved to Caerleon (the City of Legions, cited as King Arthur's court in the visionary description in Geoffrey).[8] The Bishopric of London was similarly moved to Canterbury. Brittany remained an important centre for the old British Church for a long period of time, and complex arguments about validity and authority were to develop as a result of this movement.[9]

MYTHICALLY The anecdote of the miraculous child is one usually ascribed to Christ, in a number of apocryphal stories. The reference may be to a tale of this sort, widely familiar to the medieval audience, acting as an analogue of spiritual inspiration or revelation.[10]

> 6   *A shower of blood shall rain, and a raging famine shall*
> *afflict mankind./When these things happen, the Red One*
> *shall grieve, but when his fatigue is over he shall recover his*
> *strength./Then shall misfortunes hasten upon the White One,*
> *and the buildings of his gardens be pulled down.*

HISTORICALLY This suggests plague, the other invader of Britain and of Europe at large during the middle of the sixth century.

In the latter part of this century, the advance of the Saxons into Wales was stopped by their defeat at the hands of the British.

MYTHICALLY This is our first reference to a 'shower of

blood', the feature so beloved of traditional prophecies and similar texts, but in this context it has a very literal cross-reference to the plague. The same conceit, however, may be used for several different types of event, and must be analysed in context. Many of the poetic phrases in traditional oral material are established by long usage, and can only be fully realized in their context. In a culture totally accustomed to oral transmission of knowledge and wisdom, these subtle implications would have been very obvious, particularly in a mode of recitation, where changes of pitch, tone, or subtleties of language that are impossible to express in writing, would affect the phrases concerned.[11]

When considering texts such as *The Prophecies*, this oral background must be kept in mind; it is as important as the Latin style and erudition of Geoffrey, the translator and partial creator of the work.

> 6A   *Seven who hold the Sceptre shall be killed, one of them shall become a saint.*

This refers to the Saxon kings from Cynewulf, who ascended to the throne in 757, to Ethelred who ascended in 866, and was canonized. Some translations render this line 'shall die' or 'shall perish'. (Cynewulf, Brihtric, Egbert, Ethelwulf, Ethelbald, Ethelbert, and Ethelred.)

> 7   *The bellies of mothers shall be ripped up, and infants be aborted/There shall be a most grievous punishment of men, that the natives may be restored/He that shall do these things shall be The Man of Bronze and upon a Brazen Horse shall guard the gates of London for a long time.*

HISTORICALLY The sequence of seven Kings, acting as a pivot point between one dynamic disastrous vision and another, has led us up to the ninth century. This rapid flow of events from one key vision to another is a regular feature of far-seeing, and reoccurs in several places in *The Prophecies*.

The Danes raided northern and eastern England, murdering

and plundering. King Alfred recaptured London from the Danes in 866. In the *History* we find Cadwallo (XII,13) embalmed 'and placed with wonderful art in a brazen statue . . . over the Western Gate of London . . . to be a terror to the Saxons'.

This date brings us to an interesting divergence between the traditional medieval interpretation of *The Prophecies*, and that suggested by applying a time scale with the hindsight of the twentieth century.

To Geoffrey, and to most commentators, the Prince of Brass or Bronze was Cadwallo, interred in a brazen effigy as a totem guardian against invasion. This theme, which seems rather startling in the *History*, is Geoffrey's imaginative literary re-statement of the pagan magical system of Guardianship.[12] Cadwallo acts in the same way as Bran the Blessed, whose head was interred upon the White Hill in London, to act as an Otherworld Guardian.[13]

Once again we have the problem: did Geoffrey draw the *History* from *The Prophecies*, or *The Prophecies* from the *History*? The view of the present author is that *The Prophecies*, in an oral state, predated the *History*, and that Geoffrey used them, in part, as the model for his larger work.

If this is the case, and the argument is supported only by the wealth of symbolic material, and not by any literary proof of origins, then Geoffrey wrote the relevant parts of his *History* to correspond to *The Prophecies*, albeit drawing upon many other sources to fill out and colour his narrative.

From a magical or psychological viewpoint, *The Prophecies* expand as serial time progresses; each century will add further comments and interpretation as events occur which are predicted in the text. This is not as simplistic as it seems, and although it is rationally obvious that all predictions may be forced true through time and contrivance, many of Merlin's later predicted events are startlingly correct in the modern developments of history, technology, and social change. We shall examine some of these predictions in the analysis of the second chapter of *The Prophecies*.

By way of comparison, some of the metrical verses offered by Thomas Heywood are included in an appendix. Heywood correlated *The Prophecies* up to the reign of Charles I and published his book in 1641. (See Appendix II.)

> 8   *After this the Red Dragon shall return to his proper manners, and turn his rage upon himself/ Therefore shall the revenge of The Thunderer show itself, for every field shall disappoint the husbandman/ Death shall snatch away the people, and make a desolation over all the lands.*

HISTORICALLY Crop failures and famine afflict the peoples of the Red Dragon through the divine retribution of God.

MYTHICALLY The Thunderer is one of the few direct god-names employed in our text. As a classical reference, it is Jupiter, or Jove.

> 9   *The remainder shall quit their native soil, and make foreign plantations. (as above)*

> 10   *A blessed King shall prepare a fleet, and be reckoned twelfth in the court among the Saints.*

HISTORICALLY Refers to Alfred the Great, traditionally one of the 'founders of the Navy', though this was not truly established until later centuries. His blessedness and place in the court of saints suggests Alfred's development of law, order, and learning.

> 11   *There shall be a miserable desolation of the kingdom, and the threshing floors shall become again forests/ the White Dragon shall rise again, and invite over a daughter of Germany/Our gardens shall again be replenished with foreign seed and the Red Dragon shall pine away at the end of the pool.*

HISTORICALLY Correlates to the further incursions of the Danes, and the later part of Alfred's reign. The Dane-law was created after the battle of Ethandune, along the east coast of England 'from the Thames to the Tweed'.

12   *After that shall the German Worm be crowned, and the Brazen prince will be buried/ He has his bounds assigned to him which he shall not be able to pass/ for a hundred and fifty years shall he continue in trouble and subjection, but shall bear sway three hundred.*

HISTORICALLY Canute assumes the throne in 1016. The calculations are similar to those in Gildas who wrote that the Saxons would live for 300 years in the land and would lay it waste for 150 years.

The limit for the 'Prince of Brass' is the calculation of the Saxon supremacy, from their arrival to their decline. The Saxon successes in Britain, from *c.*560 up to the late ninth century, are 330 years of 'bearing sway', while the 150 years of trouble and subjection refer to the Danes, culminating in Canute's assuming the throne.

13   *Then shall the North Wind rise against him, and shall snatch away the flowers which the West wind hath produced/There shall be gilding in the temples, but the cutting edge of the sword shall not cease to work.*

HISTORICALLY The Danes and Vikings destroy the Kingdom that Alfred once strove to create; the well endowed monasteries are laid waste.

14   *The German Dragon will hardly get to his lair, because the revenge against his treason will overtake him/ At last he shall flourish for a little time, but the decimation of Neustria will hurt him/ For a people in wood and iron coats shall come and will take vengeance for his wickedness.*

HISTORICALLY Edward the Confessor rules in comparative peace, chosen after the death of Hardecanute. In January of

1066 the last Saxon King, Harold, ascends to the throne, and is soon slain at Hastings.

The Norman conquest has begun; the Neustrians in wood and iron coats.

> 15   *They shall restore the ancient inhabitants to their dwellings, and there shall be an open destruction of foreigners/ the seed of the White Dragon shall be swept out of our gardens, and the remainder of its generation shall be decimated./ They shall bear the yoke of slavery and shall wound their mother with spades and ploughs.*

HISTORICALLY William conquers England; he engages upon social and legal reforms. He introduces a new feudal system, and the native British and Saxons are even further oppressed, pushed westwards, or made to serve as peasants.

MYTHICALLY The wounding of the mother earth may be a classical allusion, but is well in keeping with the passionate love of the land which is associated with the ancient Celts. This theme is developed later in *The Prophecies*, and comes to a dramatic conclusion in our present era, when massive abuse of the mother earth is growing commonplace.

> 16   *After this shall succeed two dragons, whereof one shall be killed with the sting of envy, but the other shall return under the cloak of authority/ Then shall succeed a Lion of Justice at whose roar the towers of Gaul and the island dragons shall tremble/ In those days gold shall be squeezed from the lily and the nettle, and silver shall flow from the hooves of bellowing cattle.*

HISTORICALLY William Rufus slain while out hunting, possibly murdered by an assassin's arrow (1100). His brother Henry returns from Normandy to rule for thirty-five years.

Henry I ruled an extensive kingdom in Europe as well as most of Britain, excluding Scotland. He raised a new taxation system from landowners.

We are now approaching the time when Geoffrey's opinions and contemporary interest begin to show clearly; there is a political element present which derives from a man writing about his own time (but as if within an ancient prophecy), and adding some of his own or his patron's wishes and hopes.

17   *Those who have frizzled hair shall put on various fleeces, and the outward habit shall denote the inward parts/ The feet of barkers shall be cut off/ Wild beasts shall enjoy peace, but mankind will bewail its punishment.*

HISTORICALLY Henry reforms the legal system. Royal hunting rights defined.

18   *The form of commerce shall be divided, and the remaining half shall be round/ The ravenousness of kits shall be destroyed, and the teeth of wolves blunted./The Lion's whelps shall be transformed into sea fishes, and an eagle shall build her nest upon mount Aravius.*

HISTORICALLY The coinage is devalued, and a new jury system is introduced. In 1120 the sinking of the White Ship caused the death of Henry's legitimate son William, and of many nobles.

MYTHICALLY The eagle building its nest upon Mount Aravius may be an allusion to a spirit of Welsh nationalism, which would have been given a boost by the confusion over the succession after the death of William. Aravius is, in fact, Snowdon.[14]

19   *Venodotia shall grow red with the blood of mothers, and the house of Corineus kill six brethren/ the island shall be wet with night tears so that all shall be provoked to all things./ Woe to thee Neustria (Normandy) because the lion's brain shall be poured upon thee, and he shall be banished with shattered limbs from his native soil.*

HISTORICALLY Henry dies at Rouen in 1135, to be succeeded by Stephen. This links also to 21 below: the civil war.

20   *Posterity shall endeavour to fly above the highest places; but the favour of newcomers shall be exalted/ Piety shall hurt the possessor of things got by impiety, till he shall have put on the raiment of his Father/ therefore, being armed with the teeth of the boar, he shall ascend above the tops of mountains and higher than the shadow of the Helmeted Man.*

HISTORICALLY Henry invades Normandy in 1106. Thus he ascends higher, in fame, than the Helmeted Man, William the Conqueror.

21   *Albania shall be enraged, and, assembling her neigh-bours, shall be employed in shedding blood/ There shall be put into her hands a bridle that shall be made on the coast of Armorica/the eagle of the broken covenant shall gild it over and rejoice in her third nest.*

HISTORICALLY The succession to the throne is disputed, Stephen claims the throne, but Scotland invades in support of Matilda. Eventually Matilda defeats Stephen, and is in turn forced to retire to Normandy in 1145. Her son, Henry II, eventually succeeds to the throne.

Geoffrey wrote the *History of the British Kings* in approximately 1135, so the events of the civil war between Stephen and Matilda were sensitive points. It may well have been this disruption of the order of kingship that prompted, in part, the writing of the work, both for reasons of Celtic nationalism (a recurring theme) and to help establish a continuity of lineage in the imagination of the noble listener. The two themes, incidentally, which seem to be self-contradictory, are intermixed in Geoffrey's work.

22   *The roaring whelps shall watch, and leaving the woods, shall hunt within the walls of the citites/ They shall make great slaughter of those that oppose them, and shall cut off the tongues of bulls/ They shall load the necks of roaring lions with chains, and restore the times of their ancestors.*

HISTORICALLY Henry II ascends to the throne in 1154. We have now reached a transition point in the text, for *The Prophecies* rapidly begin to be truly 'prophetic', in the sense that they reach a time period which could not have been described by editing through hindsight. Some of the following lines display a remarkable accuracy of prediction.

The above probably refers to the rebellion against Henry II, by his sons Henry, Geoffrey and Richard, aided by the Scots, in 1174. Henry II died in France in 1189.

23   *Then from the first to the fourth, from the fourth to the third, from the third to the second, the thumb shall roll in oil.*

This strange line marks a very significant transition into accurate prediction. If, as has often been suggested, 'rolling the thumb in oil' refers to the use of anointing oil during the ceremonial of king-making (in which the Archbishop applies consecrated oil to the proposed monarch's brow), then we have the following sequence:

    Richard I to Henry IV   1189–1413
    Henry IV to Richard III 1413–1485
    Richard III to James II 1485–1689

The line refers to the succession of monarchs which remained unbroken up to the time of James II. Charles II, curiously, though deprived of the throne during the Commonwealth had been consecrated (the thumb rolling in oil) after the execution of his father in 1649. This compression of the time-flow, which we noted earlier (Number 6 above), brings up rapidly to the reign of James I and VI.

24   *The Sixth shall overturn the walls of Ireland, and*
change the woods into a plain/He shall reduce several parts
to one, and be crowned with the head of a lion/His beginning
shall lay open to wandering affection, but his end shall carry
him up to the blessed who are above.

James VI of Scotland becomes James I of England (reducing
several parts to one etc.). He engaged upon a drastic pacification
of Northern Ireland. Despite his early wandering years and
childhood problems, he ruled surprisingly well.

25   *For he shall restore the seats of saints in their countries,*
and settle pastors in convenient places/ Two cities shall he
invest with two funeral palls, and shall bestow virgin gifts
upon virgins/ He shall merit by this the favour of the
Thunderer, and shall be placed among the saints.

HISTORICALLY We are now moving well into the future, as
far as Geoffrey's editing is concerned, and the historical keys
become more symbolic and less directly allusive or obvious.
   During the reign of James I, tithes were re-established, and in
both Wales and Ireland pastors and strengthened church
authority were promoted. The executions of the gunpowder
plotters (1605) in London, and the leaders of the rioters in
Kettering (1607), are perhaps the most notable two towns that
gained funeral palls, out of many possible candidates. As the
peasant uprising and 'the plot' were major disruptions, albeit
failed, they are likely to impinge upon the perception of the
future as nodes, or nexial points of potential and far-reaching
change.
   The colony of Virginia (virgin gifts upon virgins) was
established during James's reign, and many pastors or religious
dissenters settled there. (The first English colony in Virginia
was settled in 1607.)

MYTHOLOGICALLY We find again that divine power is
called The Thunderer, probably due to Geoffrey's classical
Latin style.

26   *From him shall proceed a lynx penetrating all things,*
who shall be bent upon the ruin of his own nation/for
through him Neustria shall lose both islands and be deprived
of its ancient dignities/ Then shall the natives return back to
the island for there shall arise a dissension among foreigners.

HISTORICALLY Charles I asserts his Divine Right, and inter-
feres with both church and parliamentary rights and reforms;
the nation takes unprecedented action. By 1660, however, the
Commonwealth had failed; Charles II was restored to the
throne. He sold Dunkirk to the French, which is probably the
loss of Neustrian (Norman) dignities, as it was one of the last
relics of the old Norman extended rule.

This sequence takes us to the abdication of James II. The
quality of the Revolution, Restoration and Abdication is
compressed into a small reference, for these were essentially
manifestations of the same inner event: a ferment leading to the
return of the White Dragon or Germanic rule, in the form of
William of Hanover.

27   *A hoary old man sitting upon a snow white horse shall*
turn the course of the River Periron, and shall measure out a
mill upon it with a white rod.

MYTHICALLY The imagery in this sentence has much in
common with a series of magical or revelatory insights. Persons
of power on white horses are seen during potent inner
perceptions of psychic reality. The image is, in fact, replete with
magical power symbols, and is one of a small number of Key
Images that mark turning points in the sequence of Prophecies.

It may be intended as a representation of the great change
arising from the deposing of the Stuarts and the incoming of
the House of Hanover – for as we saw in the earliest stages of
the sequence, leading up to Merlin's utterances, the Crown is
an expressed paradigm or focal zone for the life of the nation.
This should not be interpreted in terms of crude loyalism, but
as an ancient psychic or magical model, which derives from
very ancient cultures who held the sacred trust between land
and kingship as a central theme of their civilization. Merlin

himself is not slow to criticize royalty in *The Prophecies*, so there is no internal suggestion in our text that actual royal personalities are in any way special – they act, rather, as expressions of national consciousness, being in the driving seat of power. Much of this hardly applies today, but the magical vision of verse 27 marks a turning point in dynasties, and in the tide of British history at large.

The Key Symbols are:

> *The hoary old man*: Wisdom.
> *The White Horse*: Power. Horses were closely associated with an ancient Celtic goddess (Epona) who appears in various guises in the Mabinogion, and who may be traced in theory to the ancient carvings of Horses or Dragons that are found in the southern chalk downlands of England. In the Tarot card 'The Sun' a child is found riding upon a powerful white horse.
> *The River*: the flow of events and energies, consciousness linked to time, history.
> *The White Rod*: a magical implement of control, measurement, balance, justice.
> *The Mill*: the means of utilizing power or of manifestation. A symbol of cause and effect or interaction in the outer world.

The vision, standing alone at a historical turning point, thus reads: 'Wisdom or controlling powers of destiny, coupled to great energy and drive from the deepest sources of life will turn the course of history at this point, and upon the new course a set of far reaching interactions will be based . . . '

The 'River Periron' is one of a number of localized place names employed in *The Prophecies*, and these have to be read with caution.[15] In some cases the names are literal, while in others they are clearly functional or metaphorical. (See Appendix III for a discussion of the use of place names in *The Prophecies*.)

28   *Cadwallader shall call upon Conanus, and take Albania into alliance/ Then shall there be a slaughter of foreigners;*

then shall the rivers run with blood/Then shall break forth the fountains of Armorica, and they shall be crowned with the diadem of Brutus.

HISTORICALLY William of Orange comes to the throne in 1689, in the face of opposition from many parts of the realm, and repeated attempts to restore James to his rightful place as King.

The references to Cadwallader, Conanus, and Albany, employ the ancient kings (England, Wales, Scotland) to suggest the various plots to overthrow the German usurpers of the Crown. This revolutionary theme is again given a 'Celtic' ambience, with the 'slaughter of foreigners' and the 'fountains of Armorica'. A feature of Celtic lore is that of the fountain that erupts at a time of great importance, or the magical well that floods a land through attempts to misuse its power. There may be a hopeful suggestion of a reunion of Greater and lesser Britain (Armorica) here, a theme which was close to the hearts of the Celtic peoples.

The theme evolves, however, in the following lines (29) and may be interpreted as a vision of the remarkable development of Britain under the Hanoverians – development hallmarked by the magical image in (27) above.

29   *Cambria shall be filled with joy, and the oaks of Cornwall flourish/The island shall be called by the name of Brutus, and the name given it by foreigners shall be abolished.*

HISTORICALLY A listener of Geoffrey's day or earlier might have felt that these lines referred to a restoration of the old Celtic culture against Norman, or earlier, Saxon, oppression. Brutus, the mythological founder from whom the name of Britain was thought to be derived, was the primal ancestor of the native people in Geoffrey's *History*. Following our time scale, however, we find that by 1715 the country had reached a considerable peak of power, and that England was indeed flourishing in many ways.

When Queen Anne assumed the throne in 1702, her reign

was to mark one of the most significant events in British constitutional and social history, the Act of Union of 1707. By this Act, still unpopular today in Ireland, Scotland and Wales, the united country was officially called 'Britain', and the name 'England' was given a subsidiary place.

30   *From Conan shall proceed a war-like Boar that shall exercise the sharpness of his tusks within the Gallic woods/For he shall cut down all the larger oaks, and shall be a defence to the smaller/ The Arabians and Africans shall dread him; for he shall pursue his furious course to the further part of Spain.*

HISTORICALLY Refers to the famous Duke of Wellington, who commanded successful campaigns against the French, and also fought in Spain, Portugal, Arabia and Africa. He 'lopped down' the French Empire, and also made treaty with the 'smaller oaks' of the régime that followed. (1769-1852)

31   *Next shall succeed the Ram of the Castle of Venus, with golden horns and silver beard/He shall breathe forth a cloud from his nostrils as shall darken the surface of the Island/There shall be peace in his time, and corn shall abound by reason of the fruitfulness of the soil.*

HISTORICALLY We are now brought to the period of George IV. During his time as Prince Regent he was amorous, extravagant, and well suited to the image of Ram of Venus. He led a fashionable and flippant society, and patronized luxurious arts. These are all attributes of the Ram and Venus. In astrology, Venus in Aries implies idealism, passion, flirtation, creative power, love affairs, self-expression and generosity.

His 'cloud' of extravagance and luxurious atmosphere had difficult financial effects upon the nation following the Napoleonic war, yet the developing period of peace enabled the land to return to an attempt at balanced production. (1762-1830)

32   *Women shall become as serpents in their gait, and all
their motion shall be full of pride/The camp of Venus shall be
restored, nor shall the arrows of Cupid cease to wound/ The
fountain of a River[16] shall turn into blood, and two kings
shall fight a duel at the ford of the Staff for a Lioness.*

HISTORICALLY We are still with George III and IV. They
quarrelled violently after the Prince married a Catholic widow in
secret, and the two Kings fighting at the Ford of the Staff may
represent this dispute over the safety of the Royal power (staff
or sceptre) which was legally tied to a non-Catholic succession.

MYTHICALLY This image reminds us of the earlier measuring
rod of the old man upon a white horse; it is the staff of power.
The tone of *The Prophecies* is one of disapproval of lax morals,
and the Venerian symbolism is not a poetic conceit. Magically,
we find the sexual and generative-creative powers described
aligned to fruitful earth:

33   *Luxury shall overspread the whole ground, and fornication not cease to debauch mankind.*

The repeated link between the Ram of Venus, fornication, and
the fruitful soil is suggestive of a pagan 'Golden Age', or at
least of the ancient fertility beliefs in which the goddess of
sexual generation was also the goddess of the fruitful earth.
   This pagan quality is soon, however, to be balanced.

34   *All these things shall Three Ages see, till the buried
Kings shall be exposed to public view in the city of London.*

This line is another of the crucial pivotal sentences, by which
sections of the visionary sequence are divided. The seer has
reached a point in which there is a hiatus in his vision, and he
expresses this as a concluding phrase.
   Although we cannot fix a time scale to the Three Ages, there
are two possible divisions that fit the bill: The Three Ages
marked on our horizontal axis (Figure 1) are covered in the

prophecies that can be given a historical or factual correlation (the Heroic, Chivalric, and Transformative Ages). As these are suggested as harmonics of consciousness-through-time, they may be the three ages which the seer perceived at the summing up of this first part of his utterances. The buried Kings are exposed to public view today, in the form of being tourist attractions with little or no reverence attached to their tombs in Westminster.

A second division might be a shorter and more chronological period of 1500 years, which reaches from the presumed date of Vortigern's encounter with Merlin in the middle of the first millennium (AD 500) to the present day (AD 2000) in three stages as follows:

1 500 to the Norman Conquest (i.e. Saxons-Normans) approx. sixth to eleventh century.
2 Normans to united Crown (James I and VI) approx. eleventh to seventeenth century.
3 Struggles of Britain to twentieth century and onwards approx. seventeenth to twenty-first century.

35   *Famine shall again return/mortality shall return/and the inhabitants shall grieve for the destruction of their cities.*

HISTORICALLY we may interpret this as the close of the Regency period, but it actually performs the role of an opening sentence, following the summation above, and leads us into the next section of *The Prophecies*.

Once again, we have the paradox of the prophetic insight, certain verses have clear correlations, others do not. Some are factual, some are bardic or magical. Other lines may be from standard repertoire, of the itinerant poet or wandering seer, such as the stock lines still peddled today by so-called mediums when they are short of inspiration.

36   *Then shall come the Boar of Commerce who shall recall the scattered flocks to the pasture that they have lost/His breast shall be food to the hungry and his tongue drink to the*

thirsty/Out of his mouth shall flow rivers that shall water the parched jaws of men.

HISTORICALLY Covers the period from the middle of the eighteenth to the middle of the nineteenth centuries; the Industrial Revolution.

37   *After this shall be produced a Tree upon the Tower of London/Having no more than three branches it shall overshadow the whole Island with the breadth of its leaves/Its adversary the North Wind shall come upon it with its noxious blast, and shall snatch away the third branch.*

HISTORICALLY refers to the Royal Family. The dispute between George IV and various parties over his attempted divorce from Caroline of Brunswick, represents the battle with the North. This may also been seen as the North Wind blowing in retribution for the dissolution of the Regency and the wickedness and debauchery of George himself.[17]

The third branch snatched away is that of William IV, who died without heirs, while the remaining branch is, of course, Queen Victoria.

MYTHOLOGICALLY A repeated reference to the North Wind as the power of retribution for wickedness. In an earlier verse – 13 – the image was used to represent the Danes.

38   *The two remaining branches shall take its place, till one shall destroy another by the multitude of their leaves/This branch shall fill the place of the other two, and shall give sustenance to birds of foreign nations/ It shall be esteemed hurtful to native fowls, for they shall not be able to fly freely for fear of its shadow.*

HISTORICALLY Victoria's family was large, and intermarried with numerous foreign royal houses (German, Spanish, Prussian, Russian, Swedish, etc.). This verse actually takes us up to the creation of the present royal line, which began to appear in Victoria's reign.

There is no direct correspondence to the last line, but it follows the general tone of castigation of foreign rulers, and repeated oppression of the idealized Britons. To a medieval listener, this sequence would have obviously been a heraldic or genealogical one, and we still express family relationships as Trees today.[18]

The HISTORICAL progression now moves into a period contemporary with the present commentary. We have reached the close of a very surprising and coherent flow of prevision, which may be tied to an accurate chronology of British history without excessive intellectual juggling or wishful thinking.

The remainder of Geoffrey's Chapter 3 (Book VII) seems to lead beyond the present into a rather grim near future.

39   *Then shall succeed the Ass of Wickedness, swift against the goldsmiths, but slow against the ravenous Wolves.*

HISTORICALLY One might be tempted to see this as a reference to Hitler, and the Nazi persecution of Jews; it is rapidly conflated with another war-like or disastrous theme:

40   *In those days the oaks of the forests shall burn, and acorns grow upon lime trees/The Severn sea shall discharge itself through seven mouths, and the river Usk burn for seven months/ Fishes shall die in the heat thereof, and from them serpents will be born.*

There is no historical link for this imagery, as we have now moved into an indeterminate future. To the modern reader the description is disturbingly familar, it is the effect of nuclear accident or war. To the reader or listener of a pre-atomic age, and this means anyone prior to the explosion of the first nuclear test device, the sequence could only have been visionary or apocalyptic.

> 41   *The baths of Badon shall grow cold, and their*
> *salubrious waters engender death/London shall mourn for*
> *the death of twenty thousand, and the river Thames shall be*
> *turned to blood/ The monks in their cowls shall be forced to*
> *marry, and their cry shall be heard upon mountains of the*
> *Alps.*

While we might be inclined to pursue the connection to the
Second World War, this sequence is likely to refer to some
conflict that has not yet occurred.

To a member of a small culture with a tiny (by modern
standards) population, the death of twenty thousand people
would be an almost incomprehensible figure, particularly in the
context of familiar London.

The reference to monks may simply be an analogy of society
turned upon its head; the impossible being forced upon the
unwilling, but there may also be an element of medieval social
comment and mockery in this line.

The waters of Bath were spuriously declared 'poisonous'
1979–81, after a fatal accident in which a girl died of amoebic
meningitis. Although this may correlate to the Merlin prediction, there is conflicting medical opinion over the amoeba in the
hot springs of Bath, as these are found in all hot springs worldwide, and can only cause illness or death under very
exceptional circumstances.

The reference is more likely to be another statement of the
impossible: the revered and healing springs of hot water
turning cold, and bringing death instead of life. From (39) to
(41) we are hearing of impossible reversions of what would
have been considered firm and established realities; of horrors
that are difficult to imagine.

We shall find, towards the conclusion of the second part of
The Prophecies, that this theme is repeated, but upon a cosmic
level, with the dissolution not of nature or social order, but of
the very stars themselves.

CHAPTER 8
The second sequence:
Images beyond time

In the second phase of *The Prophecies*, the material contains a number of mystical and magical key visions. A historical analysis becomes more difficult, though there are some clearly defined images of future technology, events, and an important apocalyptic sequence.

If we follow the time scale employed previously, which has brought us up to the twentieth century by analysis of some clearly identifiable events, we find that this second phase jumps back in serial time, and finally leaps far forward of the present day.

The division is defined by Geoffrey's chapters, where the Prophecies are in Book VII, chapters 3 and 4. The sequence leading up to the disasters of the twentieth century, with the healthy Bath spring waters turning poisonous and cold, and the death toll of London's population, brings us to the close of Geoffrey's Chapter 3.

In the first part, the ominous events are British in nature, and symbolized by British places; in the second part, however, the symbolism becomes cosmic. This amplification of imagery holds true for much of Geoffrey's Chapter 4, and though we have no historical literary proof of the two-fold division, it is reasonable to conclude that the imagery and the prophetic sequences are indeed in two harmonically related parts.

This harmonic relationship, indicated by Geoffrey's chapter division, is typical of the experience of seership, and does not necessarily mean that we are encountering two separate sets of prophecies conflated or welded together for the sake of completeness. Setting aside Geoffrey's literary and propaganda requirements in his construction of the *History*, the reiteration of a historical sequence, time-jumping in both forward and reverse directions, and amplification of themes and images, are all elements well known to the seer, metaphysician or magician.

In other words, we can repeat a prophetic sequence several times with differing but harmonically related results; it cannot be pinned down to one precise and concrete structure or version.

Bearing this in mind, we can begin to examine the details of the second phase of *The Prophecies*.

42   *Three springs shall break forth in the city of Winchester, whose rivulets shall divide the island into three parts/ Whoever shall drink of the first, shall enjoy long life and never be afflicted with sickness./He that shall drink of the second, shall die of hunger and paleness and horror shall sit upon his countenance.*

43   *He that shall drink of the third, shall be surprised with sudden death, neither shall his body be capable of burial./ Those that are willing to escape so voracious a death, will endeavour to hide it with several coverings, but whatever bulk shall be laid upon it, shall receive the form of another body./For earth shall be turned into stones; stones into water; wood into ashes; ashes into water, if cast over it.*

HISTORICALLY Winchester was an important seat of power in England for several centuries, and is mentioned in both *The Prophecies* and the *History* but with a significant difference. While Geoffrey exalts Winchester in his larger work, it is eventually destroyed in *The Prophecies*. While the *History* is reflective of the author's contemporary interests, *The Prophecies* retain the matter of an oral tradition, and this to the extent of preservation even when they disagree with the political/ecclesiastical hopes of the *History*.

MYTHICALLY This vision, the precursor of the appearance of the goddess of the Land (see below), is one of those typically Celtic magical sequences, featuring springs and fountains or wells.

The primal image is one of a land which is divided into natural parts by a river or fountain flowing from its power-centre; 'Winchester' is used in this context as the allegory of a seat of power. At this stage Winchester is employed as a locus familiar to the medieval listener or reader, the hub of power expressed as the seat of kingship.

The threefold streams may be interpreted upon several different levels, and extend in symbolism beyond the primal creation-myth of a land regulated by natural divisions. Each level, however, is a harmonic of the preceding level, and this type of imagery is found in the Creation of the World poem that forms part of the *Vita Merlini* (see Appendix I). The Creation verses are based upon the Fourfold Elements, while our present example is triadic.

The verses reflect an ancient tradition: that of the Three Mothers, here symbolized by Life, Hunger, and Death. The threefold division of the island of Britain becomes an allegory of the human life and polarities of consciousness, via the cyclical pattern of inner powers, or the mysterious life-death cycle. (Figure 4)

The description of the effects of the Three Streams is closely paralleled by a number of wisdom tales and magical images.[1] They are also reminiscent of instructions to the soul, not in this case the soul after death, but the soul seeking to enter birth.[2] *The water of long life and health* is that of Wisdom, the power of the Goddess of Blessing.

The water of insatiable hunger is that of Consuming, or lust, an imbalance of the water of life. This is the power of the Goddess of Cursing. A curse takes a beneficial power and twists it into a negative polarity, turning good into destruction.

The water of sudden death is that of Annihilation, the end of the threefold-cycle, the power of the Goddess of Taking. It is significant, that this third power is represented by sudden death without burial and that burial becomes an impossibility. To both the medieval Christian and to the pagan Celt, a body rejected by the earth meant not only physical death, but spiritual death, without hope of Resurrection or Rebirth.[3]

This rather grim cycle of life and death, founded upon a very ancient concept still used in modern meditation and magical work, is the basis for poetic systems such as those outlined by Robert Graves in his famous work *The White Goddess*.[4]

In modern revival occult groups, a rather cosy three-fold

THE THREE FOUNTAINS

LIFE

DEATH

DESIRE

Goddess imagery is employed, lacking the inevitability and impersonal power of the primal Three Mothers.[5] (Figure 5) 'Those wishing to escape so great a surfeit (or so voracious a death-fit), will endeavour to hide it with several coverings.' The deeper element of the inner-being, the seeds of death inherent in the cycle of life, are covered by successive layers of the psyche, and in magical terminology, by the expression of the spirit and psyche as the outer physical body.

'Whatsoever substance is placed on top will immediately take on the form of another substance . . . ' This sequence could well be a restatement of a modern text on psychology, once again we are reminded of alchemical symbolism. The transubstantiation of different layers piled upon the spring of death, is a description of our own psychic and magical nature. We continually attempt to disguise the inevitable truth from ourselves, like Vortigern and his Tower, but as fast as we attempt to cover up our perception of potential death, so do our façades change substance as the fountains beneath make their potent influence felt.

'Earth will be turned into stones, stones into water, wood into ashes, and ash into water . . . '

This line deals with the primal elements, and is reminiscent of a number of children's games, based upon similar changes of substance. Possibly the entire sequence is the remnant of a Mystery teaching regarding transubstantiation within the cycle of Birth-Lifetime-Death.

Alchemy was particularly concerned with the application of the Elements (Air, Fire, Water, and Earth) in a pattern that altered the seemingly inevitable cycles, and created a new substance – the Philosopher's Stone. This in turn had the inherent power of beneficial transubstantiation, changing whatever it touched 'into gold'. It may be significant that in each of the changes described, Fire is the active agent. The application of heat, or the combustion of a substance, will effect each of the visible changes in the sequence, in a series of simple experiments which can be carried out under basic laboratory conditions. Experiments of this sort played an important role in the wisdom systems embodied in medieval and later alchemy, in which the physical reactions were understood to be analogues of other and metaphysical events.[6]

THE THREE MOTHERS

As a result of the basic law of magic, in which physical events are analogues of metaphysical events, the apparently simplistic repetition of basic combustion and evaporation experiments takes on a fresh value. Ancient teachings such as those embodied in fragmentary form in *The Prophecies* are not merely psychic allegories, they also represent the physical/ magical operations which eventually became re-expressed in the alchemical literature. If we presume that the Merlin text pre-dates Geoffrey, at least in its oral source, we may see it as one of the earliest native alchemical text books.

Curiously, the symbols do not include the Arabic influence which plays so great a role in medieval alchemy. As we shall see later Merlin's vision of the end of time is based upon ancient Greek symbolism combined with Celtic mythology, and the astrology is not Arabic but Greek. This lack of Arabic influence would tend to support the theory that *The Prophecies* are an early oral text incorporated by Geoffrey without a great deal of tampering.[7]

From a primal geomantic-psychic threefold map, Merlin now moves on to a graphic and powerful description of the Goddess of the Land of Britain.

44 *Also a damsel shall be sent from the city of the forest of Canute* (or the city of the hoary forest), *to administer a cure/ Once she has practised her oracular arts, she shall dry up the noxious fountains by breathing upon them./Afterwards, as soon as she shall refresh herself with the wholesome liquor, she shall bear in her right hand the wood of Caledon, and in her left the buttressed forts of London.*

MYTHICALLY We are being offered a description of a goddess, a vision of potency that represents the land, and the essential powers of transformation inherent within the spirit of the earth. This is the Goddess of Britain, who appears again in a later sequence under the name of Ariadne, when she takes on a cosmic rather than a localized manifestation.

She comes from a city in an ancient forest ('Canuti nemoris'), and as such is the forerunner of some of the visionary sequences in the Grail legends which flourished shortly after

Geoffrey's *History* was 'published' or copied. Both derive from an oral tradition, and the imaginative picture is as follows:

(A) *Deep in an ancient wild forest, is a magical and holy city. Within the city dwells a virgin of magical power, attuned to the land. She is able to foretell the future, and is the keeper of three springs (Life, Desire, Death). Only when she is approached may the seeker after Life drink of the correct spring, for it is her breath that dries up the sources of Desire and Death.*

From this first magical image, which provides the keys to an inner alchemy in which the sexual energies are transformed into a higher mode of operation through meditation, visualization, and invocation, we move to a second more outward expression of the same magical goddess image.

During her 'drying of the noxious springs', the maiden loses her energy, but upon drinking from 'the wholesome liquor' she takes on a new appearance – she becomes the land in visualized manifestation; holding the forest of Scotland and the fortresses of London in either hand, her power extends from North to South, from wilderness to civilization.

45   *Wherever she shall go, she shall make sulphurous steps, which shall smoke with a double flame./That smoke shall rouse up the Ruteni, and shall make food for the inhabitants of the deep sea./ Tears of compassion will overflow her eyes, and she shall fill the island with dreadful cries.*

MYTHICALLY The goddess is active in the environment, her power is so great that her footsteps burst into flame, an image of vigour often applied to pagan deities. By her fiery arousal of the earth, she awakens ancient tribes (the Ruteni), and nourishes the creatures that live in the depths.

This imagery is very similar to that of the closing section of *The Prophecies*, where Ariadne in her underground refuge presides over the arousal of the Ancestors, while the land sinks under the waves (Chapter 10). We are being offered our first vision of the Goddess who presides over the three-fold nature of creation: 1) the individual life; 2) the life of the land; 3) the life of the planet and solar system.

During the closing visionary sequences, we shall encounter her again in her third and most terrifying aspect, where the ordered universe seen from the Earth is set into chaotic ferment. To continue our visualization:

(B) *The maiden has given her energies to counteract the negative powers of the poisoned springs, but on drinking of the waters of Life, she takes on a new mature expression. Holding a fortress in one hand, and a forest in the other, she walks across the land, and in her wake the spirits of the ancient people awaken, and the deepest primal life forms are nourished by her potency. She weeps with compassion for the sufferings of her people. She is transformed from a virgin of purity to a mature and suffering Mother.*

The power of this pagan imagery is undeniable; this is the vision of the Mother Goddess, known by countless names throughout the world. She is the archetype (in the true sense of the word) of all the mysterious Queens and Maidens in the Grail legends and the Celtic tales, women of power who control the secret energies by which the hero gains his quest.

46 *She shall be killed by a hart with ten branches, four of which shall bear golden diadems; but the other six shall be turned into the horns of oxen, whose hideous bellowing shall arouse the three islands of Britain.*

MYTHICALLY This image is similar to a number of traditional symbols relating to polarity, and particularly to the state of consciousness known in orthodox religion as 'the fall from Grace'.

A hart with ten branches (stag with ten tines) is a power or energy image, and while four of the branches are crowned, which means spiritually balanced and fulfilled, the six remaining branches are units of unbalanced force. We find similar descriptions in other mystical images: the Tree of Life used in modern magical work employs ten stages or 'spheres' of creative manifestation. In this image the upper three spheres (The Crown, Wisdom and Understanding) are 'crowned', while the remaining seven gravitate towards the fallen state of Earth, the Tenth and First Sphere.[8]

The hideous bellowing of the oxen represents their state of imbalance and destruction. It is tempting to align this vision with a sequence of royal succession, in which four good rulers are counterbalanced by six destructive ones; or perhaps we might suggest four periods of satisfactory government set against six of oppression and discord.

The invocation of the Goddess now ceases, and as is often the case within *The Prophecies* (as in many traditional verses and tales) we make an instant transition to the next phase. We now descend from the heady poetry of magical sight and incantation, into the historical or semi-historical predictive element. This rise and fall of consciousness is typical of prophetic writings, or sayings, and has been fully described in our earlier chapters.

Just as the first phase of *The Prophecies* opened with the allegory of the Tower, and the Arousal of the Dragons, so does the second phase open with a description of the primal Kingdom, and its Queen the Goddess of The Land. In both cases, the power symbolism is immediately followed by a predictive sequence.

47   *The Daneian wood shall be stirred up, and breaking forth into a human voice shall cry: 'Come O Cambria, bring Cornwall at your side, and say to Winchester, the earth shall swallow you up! Translate the see of your pastor to the place where the ships come to harbour, and the rest of the limbs shall follow the head. For the day approaches when your citizens shall perish on account of the guilt of perjury. The whiteness of wool has been hurtful to you, and the variety of its tinctures. Woe to the perjured nation, for whom the city shall be ruined*

HISTORICALLY A distinct element of pan-Celtic nationalism now appears, following directly upon the invocation of the Goddess of the Land. This sequence refers directly to the argument about the supremacy fo the see of St David's. As we have mentioned this dispute in several places, it is worth summarizing, with its relevance to *The Prophecies* in general. If this sequence does not mention Menevia (St David's) as such, the sense of the passage would certainly remind the reader or listener of this well known dispute for power, best represented to us today by Gerald of Wales in his constant striving to re-establish the ancient Welsh see as the metropolitan seat of Wales.[9]

In about AD 550 St Samson fled Wales, for Dol in Brittany, reputedly taking the pallium with him. St David's traditional status as the seat of an independent archbishop, connected to the old Celtic Church, was still disputed in the time of Geoffrey and of course by Gerald, who turned down other preferments in the hope of gaining St David's. The attempts to make the Welsh church independent from Canterbury failed.

The appeal for a withdrawal of power from Winchester to 'where the ships come to harbour' is clearly part of the Celtic nationalistic feeling expressed earlier, where the Daneian wood (Forest of Dean) incites Wales and Cornwall to unite and curse Winchester.

MYTHICALLY This sequence adopts the hectoring tone familiar from the Old Testament prophets, and indeed from Jesus, in which corruption is openly criticized, and revolution openly encouraged. The mystical and political elements are inseparable.

49   *The ships shall rejoice at such a great augmentation, and one shall be made out of two.*

50   *It shall be rebuilt by a Hedgehog laden with apples, to the smell of which birds will flock from different woods./He shall add to it a vast palace walled around with six hundred towers./ Therefore shall London envy it, and triply increase her walls.*

HISTORICALLY Refers to the competition between Winchester and London as a seat for royal power and privilege, but should not be taken too literally, as it leads to a vision that seems to apply directly to the present day:

51   *The river Thames shall encompass London, and the*
fame of this work shall pass beyond the Alps/ The Hedgehog
shall hide his apples within it, and shall make subterraneous
passages./At that time shall the stones speak, and the area
towards the Gallic coast be contracted into a narrow
space./On each bank shall one man hear another, and the
soil of the island shall be enlarged./The secrets of the deep
shall be revealed, and Gaul shall tremble for fear.

HISTORICALLY   Correlates well with present day London,
which is not 'encompassed' by the Thames, but does have a
remarkable tidal barrier that prevents water damage. The city is
also permeated with subterraneous passages, and the wealth of
the nation (the Hedgehog's apples) is linked to the city's role as
a finance centre. (In Thorpe, however, this line is cross-referred
to Winchester and not to London.)

The present era could well be described as the time of
speaking stones: our new technology is based upon the quartz
crystal, the microchip for computers, which is literally a
speaking stone. The diminishing space between England and
France suggests our present instantaneous modes of communication, employing the 'speaking stones', by which men on
either shore may hear one another. We might even suggest that
the enlarging of the island's soil refers to the North Sea oil and
gas exploration and development, by which the secrets of the
deep are indeed revealed.

MYTHICALLY   This symbolism is once again reminiscent of
the recurring theme of rising lands or changing seas, by which
secrets are revealed. We may take this as a psychological model
in addition to offering its correlation to present day technology.
In the prophetic consciousness, both manifestations are derived
from the same fundamental source.

We now enter upon the most obscure passage in the text, one
which poses apparently insoluble problems, particularly if we
insist on a predictive or pseudo-factual interpretation.

A number of magical images are contained in this long
section of transformations, and as these are in keeping with the
style of symbolism analysed in our earlier interpretations, many
of them will need no further elucidation.

VISUAL CONTENT

The most striking feature of this sequence is the flow of visual images; they merge into one another with great rapidity. The implication is that of a traditional sequence of verses which has been set out intact.

Shape-changing is found in many folk tales, legends, chronicles and early histories, but none as chaotic as that offered by Merlin. Before setting out to examine briefly some of the contents of this part of *The Prophecies*, we should consider the circumstances under which it might have arisen.

As has been suggested earlier, the second chapter of the text contains some recondite themes and images, and seems to reach far into the future. The first chapter, however, has a firm time scale, and many more identifiable historical correlations. Our second section contains a very large number of animal images, and as the precedent for animals representing historical persons has been well established, we may assume that this is the case in parts 51-85. No hindsight has been edited into these lines by Geoffrey, as has obviously occurred in the earlier lines of the first chapter of prophetic utterances.

While we may not reach a satisfactory solution to the problem of correlating this part of the text with historical events, we can at least attempt to understand the circumstances under which the seer has uttered these lines.

ANIMAL SYMBOLISM

The panoply of animals represents persons, usually royal or influential, who may have appeared to the inner eye. The names and historical position are not known to the seer, for they are in his 'future', but he can perceive the effect that they generate, an interaction which is symbolized to his inner eye by the complex sequence of animals, shape changes, conflicts and retributions.

It must be emphasized that this model is justified, even if we are not encountering actual examples of seership. The methods of prophecy produce results similar to those found in our text, and the imagery of native British prophecy is the imagery here encountered. It is different in many respects from that of Biblical prophecy, and strongly reminiscent of descriptions that were to arise in a later century during the trials of so-called 'witches'.

The animals are also representative of qualities: the Heron who is the queen of all birds (51), the cunning fox and wolf, the strong boar (53 and 54). They are therefore people of influence in history, who are similar in their qualities to the animals described. We have examples of this that may be correlated within Geoffrey's own historical period, found in the earlier prophecies. (see Chapter 7)

SERPENT AND DRAGON

The Serpent acts both as an animal symbolizing a human quality (66 in which the serpent of Malvern follows the raven, kites, and the owl of Gloucester) and in a greater role, as magical and terrifying creature (67). The Dragon has a similar two-fold role, as in the Dragon of Worcester (68) which at first seems to be a person, but soon develops as a vision of greater intensity.

MAGICAL IMAGES

Scattered among the parade of unknown persons and fluid shape-changing creatures, are a number of precise magical images. These stand out clearly amidst the bulk of the imagery, and are easy to find by the very nature of their poetic and visual quality and strength.

58   In her days shall a Serpent be brought forth, which shall be a destroyer of mankind. With its length it shall encompass London, and devour all that pass by it.

67   In his days shall the Pachaian mountains tremble, and the provinces be deprived of their woods. For there shall come a worm with a fiery breath, and with the vapour it sends forth shall burn up the trees. Out of it shall proceed seven lions deformed with the heads of goats . . .

68 ... Then shall come the giant of wickedness, and terrify all with the sharpness of his eyes. Against him shall rise the Dragon of Worcester, and shall endeavour to banish him.

69 But in the engagement the dragon shall be worsted, and oppressed by the wickedness of the conqueror. For he shall mount upon the dragon, and putting off his garment shall sit upon him naked. The dragon shall bear him up on high, and beat his naked rider with his tail erected. Upon this the giant rousing up his whole strength shall break his jaws with his sword. At last the dragon shall fold itself up under its tail, and die of poison.

74 ... Thus being naked shall he overcome him, whom when clothed he was not able to deal with.

76 The giant of the snow-white colour shall shine, and cause the white people to flourish. Pleasures shall effeminate the princes, and they shall suddenly be changed into beasts.

77 ... A charioteer of York shall appease them, and having banished his lord, shall mount upon the chariot which he shall drive. With his sword unsheathed shall he threaten the East, and fill the tracks of his wheels with blood.

82 ... One shall come in armour, and shall ride upon a flying serpent. He shall sit upon his back with his naked body, and cast his right hand upon his tail. With his cry shall the seas be moved, and he shall strike terror. . .

86 A man shall embrace a lion in wine, and the dazzling brightness of gold shall blind the eyes of beholders. . .

87 From them shall the Stars turn away their faces, and confound their usual course. Corn will wither at their malign aspects, and there shall fall no dew from Heaven. . .

These remarkable images are quite at odds with the general tone of *The History*, and hardly seem typical of Geoffrey's polished and rather relaxed stretches of imagination expressed throughout his British book. We can only assume that he took them down verbatim, or nearly so, from some hallowed oral source. Despite the apparent chaos of the images, there are recurring motifs which are worth elaboration.

THE NAKED GIANT AND THE DRAGON

The repeated image of the naked giant fighting a dragon is something which occurs by implication in the astrology of the concluding phase of *The Prophecies*: the vision of the end of time. As we shall see in our next chapter, the mythical hunter Orion, a giant stellar figure of importance to the ancients, is said to be in conflict with the constellation of Scorpio. Due to their relative positions in the night sky, Orion appears to be fleeing Scorpio. The images listed above imply a conflict between Orion and Scorpio, for there is no doubt that the Dragon is of a scorpion-like nature. Thorpe translates this line as 'finally the dragon shall become entangled in its own tail and will die of poison.'

The Naked Giant battling the Dragon is redolent of primal titanic struggles, expressed in star-lore as the figures of Orion and Scorpio, and in later myths as the hero who slays a monster, or Saint George and the Dragon. We are encountering a very early and basic expression of this theme when we meet it in repeated imagery in *The Prophecies*.

THE INVERSION OF NATURAL ORDER

Inversion is another repeated pattern in the text; the Valley of Galabes (Merlin's personal haunt, containing a magical fountain) becomes a mountain. Many of the creatures exhibit characteristics of inversion: birds flocking together to destroy mankind, multiple beasts with grotesque features, lions that corrupt women into prostitution, the Pachaian mountains tottering, and so forth.

In many ways this lengthy passage prepares us for the clearly defined scheme that occurs at the close of the vision: the end of the solar system and the elemental patterns of creation. We might regard this ferment of disturbing imagery as a first boiling up of the inner energies, the purgation, prior to the dissolution that follows.

Whatever 'meaning' interpreters may put upon these lines, there can be no doubt that they lead to the awesome final vision, and that their dramatic effect is to build tension and readiness for the moment when 'root and branch change places'.

51A After these things shall come forth a heron from the forest of Calaterium, which shall fly round the island for two years together. With her nocturnal cry she shall call together the winged kind, and assemble to her all sorts of fowls. They shall invade the tillage of husbandmen, and devour all the grain of the harvests. 52 Then shall follow a famine upon the people, and a grievous mortality upon the famine. But when this calamity shall be over, a detestable bird shall go to the valley of Galabes, and shall raise it to be a high mountain. Upon the top thereof it shall also plant an oak, and build its nest in its branches. Three eggs shall be produced in the nest, from whence shall come forth a fox, a wolf, and a bear. 53 The fox shall devour her mother, and bear the head of an ass. In this monstrous form shall she frighten her brothers, and make them fly into Neustria. But they shall stir up the tusky boar, and returning in a fleet shall encounter with the fox; who at the beginning of the fight shall feign herself dead, and move the boar to compassion. 54 Then shall the boar approach her carcass, and standing over her, shall breathe upon her face and eyes. But she, not forgetting her cunning, shall bite his left foot, and pluck it off from his body. Then shall she leap upon him, and snatch away his right ear and tail, and hide herself in the caverns of the mountains. 55 Therefore shall the deluded boar require the wolf and bear to restore him his members; who, as soon as they shall enter into the cause, shall promise two feet of the fox, together with the ear and tail, and of these they shall make up the members of a hog. 56 With this he shall be satisfied, and expect the promised restitution. In the meantime shall the fox descend from the mountains, and change herself into a wolf, and under pretence of holding a conference with the boar, she shall go to him, and craftily devour him. 57 After that she shall transform herself into a boar, and feigning a loss of some members, shall wait for her brothers; but as soon as they are come, she shall suddenly kill them with her tusks, and shall be crowned with the head of a lion. 58 In her days shall a serpent be brought forth, which shall be a destroyer of mankind. With its length it shall encompass London, and devour all that pass by it. 59 The mountain ox shall take the head of a wolf, and whiten his teeth in the Severn. He shall gather to him the flocks of Albania and Cambria, which shall drink the river Thames dry. 60 The ass shall call the goat with the long beard, and shall borrow his shape. Therefore shall the mountain ox be incensed, and having called the wolf, shall become a horned bull against them. In the exercise of his cruelty he shall devour their flesh and bones, but shall be burned upon the top of Urian. 61 The ashes of his funeral-pile shall be turned into swans, that shall swim on dry ground as on a river. They shall devour fishes in fishes, and swallow up men in men. 62 But when old age shall come upon them, they shall become sea-wolves, and practise their frauds in the deep. They shall drown ships, and collect no small quantity of silver. 63 The Thames shall again flow, and assembling together the rivers, shall pass beyond the bounds of its channel. It shall cover the adjacent cities, and overturn the mountains that oppose its course. 64 Being full of deceit and wickedness, it shall make use of the fountain Galabes. Hence shall arise factions provoking the Venedotians to war. The oaks of the forest shall meet together, and encounter the rocks of the Gewisseans. 65 A raven shall attend with the kites, and devour the carcasses of the slain. An owl shall build her nest upon the walls of Gloucester, and in her nest shall be brought forth an ass. 66 The serpent of Malvernia shall bring him up, and put him upon many fraudulent practices. Having taken the crown, he shall ascend on high, and frighten the people of the country with his hideous braying. 67 In his days shall the Pachaian mountains tremble, and the provinces be deprived of their woods. For there shall come a worm with a fiery breath, and with the vapour it sends forth shall burn up the trees. Out of it shall proceed seven lions deformed with the heads of goats. With the stench of their nostrils they shall corrupt women, and make wives turn common prostitutes. 68 The father shall not know his own son, because they shall grow wanton like brute beasts. Then shall come the giant of wickedness, and terrify all with the sharpness of his eyes. Against him shall arise the dragon of Worcester, and shall endeavour to banish him. 69

But in the engagement the dragon shall be worsted, and oppressed by the wickedness of the conqueror. For he shall mount upon the dragon, and putting off his garment shall sit upon him naked. The dragon shall bear him up on high, and beat his naked rider with his tail erected. Upon this the giant rousing up his whole strength, shall break his jaws with his sword. At last the dragon shall fold itself up under its tail, and die of poison. 70 After him shall succeed the boar of Totness, and oppress the people with grievous tyranny. Gloucester shall send forth a lion, and shall disturb him in his cruelty, in several battles. He shall trample him under his feet, and terrify him with open jaws. 71 At last the lion shall quarrel with the kingdom, and get upon the backs of the nobility. A bull shall come into the quarrel, and strike the lion with his right foot. He shall drive him through all the inns in the kingdom, but shall break his horns against the walls of Oxford. 72 The fox of Kaerdubalem shall take revenge on the lion, and destroy him entirely with her teeth. She shall be encompassed by the adder of Lincoln, who with a horrible hiss shall give notice of his presence to a multitude of dragons. 73 Then shall the dragons encounter, and tear one another to pieces. The winged shall oppress that which wants wings, and fasten its claws into the poisonous cheeks. Others shall come into the quarrel, and kill one another. 74 A fifth shall succeed those that are slain, and by various stratagems shall destroy the rest. He shall get upon the back of one with his sword, and sever his head from his body. Then throwing off his garment, he shall get upon another, and put his right and left hand upon his tail. Thus being naked shall he overcome him, whom when clothed he was not able to deal with. 75 The rest he shall gall in their flight, and drive them round the kingdom. Upon this shall come a roaring lion dreadful for his monstrous cruelty. Fifteen parts shall he reduce to one, and shall alone possess the people. 76 The giant of the snow-white colour shall shine, and cause the white people to flourish. Pleasures shall effeminate the princes, and they shall suddenly be changed into beasts. 77 Among them shall arise a lion swelled with human gore. Under him shall a reaper be placed in the standing corn, who, while he is reaping, shall be oppressed by him. A charioteer of York shall appease them, and having banished his lord, shall mount upon the chariot which he shall drive. With his sword unsheathed shall he threaten the East, and fill the tracks of his wheels with blood. 78 Afterwards he shall become a sea-fish, who, being roused up with the hissing of a serpent, shall engender with him. From hence shall be produced three thundering bulls, who having eaten up their pastures shall be turned into trees. The first shall carry a whip of vipers, and turn his back upon the next. 79 He shall endeavour to snatch away the whip, but shall be taken by the last. They shall turn away their faces from one another, till they have thrown away the poisoned cup. 80 To him shall succeed a husbandman of Albania, at whose back shall be a serpent. He shall be employed in ploughing the ground, that the country may become white with corn. The serpent shall endeavour to diffuse his poison, in order to blast the harvest. 81 A grievous mortality shall sweep away the people, and the walls of cities shall be made desolate. There shall be given for a remedy the city of Claudius, which shall interpose the nurse of the scourger. For she shall bear a dose of medicine, and in a short time the island shall be restored. 82 Then shall two successively sway the sceptre, whom a horned dragon shall serve. One shall come in armour, and shall ride upon a flying serpent. He shall sit upon his back with his naked body, and cast his right hand upon his tail. With his cry shall the seas be moved, and he shall strike terror into the second. 83 The second therefore shall enter into confederacy with the lion; but a quarrel happening, they shall encounter one another. They shall distress one another, but the courage of the beast shall gain the advantage. 84 Then shall come one with a drum, and appease the rage of the lion. Therefore shall the people of the kingdom be at peace, and provoke the lion to a dose of physic. In his established seat he shall adjust the weights, but shall stretch out his hands into Albania. For which reason the northern provinces shall be grieved, and open the gates of the temples. 85 The sign-bearing wolf shall lead his troops, and surround Cornwall with his tail. He shall be opposed by a soldier in a chariot, who shall transform that people into a boar. The boar shall therefore ravage the provinces, but shall hide his head in the depth of Severn. 86

A man shall embrace a lion in wine, and the dazzling brightness of gold shall blind the eyes of beholders. Silver shall whiten in the circumference, and torment several wine presses. Men shall be drunk with wine, and regardless of heaven, shall be intent upon the earth. 87 From them shall the Stars turn away their faces and confound their usual course. Corn will wither at their malign aspects, and there shall fall no dew from Heaven.

CHAPTER 9
The apocalyptic vision:
Stellar and psychic transformation

(88) A. *Root and branch shall change places, and the newness of the thing shall pass as a miracle/ The brightness of the Sun shall fade at the amber of Mercury, and horror shall seize the beholders./ Stilbon of Arcadia shall change his shield; the Helmet of Mars shall call Venus.*

(89) *The Helmet of Mars shall make a shadow; and the rage of Mercury shall exceed its orbit./Iron Orion shall unsheathe his sword; the marine Phoebus shall torment the clouds/ Jupiter shall go out of his lawful paths; and Venus forsake her appointed circuits.*

(90) *The malignity of the star Saturn shall fall down in rain, and slay mankind with a crooked sickle./ The Twelve Houses of the Stars shall lament the irregular excursions of their inmates.*

These lines open one of the most remarkable sections of the entire *Prophecies*, the vision that reaches to the end of time. This dramatic vision also encapsulates the actual psychic and magical ferment that is represented outwardly by the prophetic utterances.

The final vision, therefore, is on a number of levels both personal and individual, and collective and ultimately universal. The chaos of the inner energies, the Aroused Dragons, brings the fundamental powers up from beneath the earth, or from the hidden depths of the consciousness. While examining this material, we must constantly bear in mind the Hermetic axiom: 'As above, so below', for each astrological event is a mirror of a psychic interaction.

The fact that the images are chaotic and disruptive is not an implication of 'evil', but of powers that alter the fabric of established conceptualization. To grasp this imagery fully, we must consider some of the literary, cultural, and initiatory background from which it derives.

(A) The passage opens with the words '*Root and branch shall change places*'. In a number of places in the text, the normal relative directions or positions are exchanged: the valley of Galabes becomes a mountain, the hills are laid low, the seas narrow and the lands increase, and so forth. This reversal of accepted direction or proportion is central to all inner development, and is found specifically in systems that alter consciousness by catalytic or even cathartic methods. Such systems include shamanism, Tibetan Buddhism, Tantric yoga, and the genuine magical traditions of the west. We find them also in the primitive initiations of the Indian tribes, and in the primal symbolism of Norse mythology.

To illustrate the Merlin text, however, we have a native tradition of considerable importance, that of the UnderWorld Journey, and the Inverted Tree.

One of the key symbols of the British catalytic system of magic, is an inverted Tree, growing into Faeryland or the Otherworld which is beneath the earth. It is this realm that supplies the magical fountains, such as that of Galabes where Merlin is found, for it is the source of all primal power that emerges into the upper world. This symbolism is not only an analogy of the human consciousness, it also extends into metaphysical realms and laws which are not admitted into modern psychology, such as the powerful relationship between humankind and the energies of the land.

Merlin prefaces his final vision, therefore, with a key phrase: '*Root and branch shall change places.*' This identifying image advises us that we are about to hear something from the deepest UnderWorld; to the initiate, the changing of root and branch for one another has a specific magical meaning relating to polarity of consciousness and sexual energy. This subject, well represented in eastern texts on meditation and yoga, has been suppressed and glossed over in the west due to orthodox influence from the Churches.

Obscure works, such as the Grail texts, and the Merlin texts of *The Prosphecies* and the *Vita*, abound with technical magical instruction, and merely require a new level of interpretation and elucidation into modern language to become operative.

The image of root and branch refers not only to a genuine and irrevocable reversal of direction of attention (ie inward instead of outward, downward instead of upward growth) but also refers to the change of flow of the sensual energies. In magic and in meditation, the catalytic changes are partly energized by drawing the sexual or bio-electrical energies up through the body. This Arousal of the Inner Fire stimulates a number of centres of biological and psychic importance, and eventually 'reaches the brain', where it acts as a super-catalyst for consciousness, and according to esoteric teaching effects small but significant changes in the pineal gland and in the bloodstream.[1]

At the very beginning of *The Prophecies*, we saw this arousal in the form of a Red and White Dragon; at the close we encounter it in the exchange of root and branch.

'*The newness of the thing shall pass as a miracle.*' We find similar phrases in orthodox religion, derived from the Book of Revelation which has possibly influenced some of the Merlin text. 'And I saw a new heaven and a new earth; for the first heaven and the first earth are passed away; and the sea is no more' (Revelation 21,1).

But despite an apparently Biblical phrase, representing that which is commonly experienced by people attaining an insight or unusual change of consciousness, we immediately proceed to astrological and quite pagan symbolism. In the medieval period, astrology was not frowned upon as 'magical', though it later fell into disrepute. There is not, therefore, anything unusual about the use of astrological symbolism in a set of verses written down during the twelfth century.

There are two important classical or pseudo-classical references which have coloured Geoffrey's text, though this does not prove that the original concepts were borrowed wholesale from classical writings. We shall also find that the astrology is Greek, and not Arabic as one might expect. This internal evidence contributes to the theory that the *Prophecies of Merlin* are an old text, older than the general composition of much of the *History* itself.

Before delving into the magical or psychological depths of the lines themselves, we must consider the classical and astrological sources, which are literary in the historical or derivative sense. The literary derivation, however, is not conclusive proof by any means that Geoffrey fabricated *The Prophecies* from his wide reading and classical education. Assuming that there is a genuine element to traditional prophetic insight, and to the wisdom teachings of the ancients (however we may choose to define this element), it is likely that both classical 'sources' and native symbolism derive from the same unwritten core tradition – not a secret teaching as such, but a regenerative mode of consciousness.

It is only in the light of this central consciousness that a true understanding of *The Prophecies* may be obtained; if we find evidence that certain Greek and Roman philosophical attitudes are mirrored in the British visions, then it is because these attitudes are the common property of the consciousness of western man, and not because one borrowed textually or even verbally from the other.

LITERARY SOURCES

The tone of the concluding vision of Merlin is similar to Lucan's *Pharsalia*, Book I. The *Pharsalia* describes the civil war between Caesar and Pompey, and was written in the middle part of the first century AD. In this first book, the Romans consult the omens. The seer Figulus reports that either the stars have broken their natural laws or that mankind is headed for ruin.

Geoffrey was familiar with Lucan, and quotes from the *Pharsalia* (II,572) in the *History* (*Hist*.IV,9), where he mentions Lucan also in other contexts. The cosmology of the Merlin vision, according to Tatlock,[2] is similar to that of classical Stoic philosophy, but it bears marked similarities to other cosmological systems also, and should not be assumed to derive from entirely classical sources.

Another literary source, popular during Geoffrey's day, was the *Oracula Sibyllina*, written during the first century AD. The currency of this text was part of the medieval passion for prophecies in general. A number of Biblical parallels may be cited: Rev. VI,13; Rev. XII,4; Isaiah XIII,10; Mark XIII,24-25.

These sources set the tone for the literary expression of Geoffrey's adaptation of his sources, and they were undoubtedly in his mind or available to him at the time of his writing, plus other possible sources that are now lost. The general ambience of cataclysmic vision, however, is not a literary inheritance, but an inner property of human consciousness, whether it is based upon orthodoxy, propaganda, fear, or genuine prevision.

The standpoint of the present author is that the literary parallels prove a general stream of symbolism, and not the case for Geoffrey concocting *The Prophecies* as a clever exercise based upon his own reading.

ASTROLOGICAL MATERIAL

The astrological theme of Merlin's vision is firmly stated: the planets move out of their appointed circuits and, as we shall see in the development of the sequence, behave in a manner that is the opposite of their accustomed attributes. This behaviour is described in detail, with a practical astrological and cosmological scheme behind the actions of the planets.

In this detail, the vision far exceeds the orthodox Biblical references, in which the images are generally poetic and not technically defined. In the Biblical examples listed above, the stars fall from the sky, or the Sun is obscured, but by Merlin we are told of specific stars having specific effects. We shall return to the details of this astrology as we progress further into the last vision. At this stage we may draw from Tatlock, who points out that a relationship between Mercury and amber is a Greek astrological attribute. 'Stilbon of Arcadia' (verse 88) is a directly Greek term, as the word 'stilbon' is Greek for 'glittering'.[3]

This Greek emphasis, reinforced in later lines by comparison between Ariadne and the native goddess encountered at the opening of Chapter II of *The Prophecies*, implies that the astrology was defined before the influx of Arabic lore from medieval Spain, an influx which was directly contemporary with Geoffrey, and with which he must have been familiar. Indeed, his vision of the gathering of astrologers at Arthur's court at Caerleon is partly based upon accounts of Spanish/ Moslem seats of philosophy.[4]

The astrological exchanges, however, are not merely inherited; they are a product of consciousness, and provide us with the main key to the prophetic consciousness itself.

THE DRAGON'S HEAD AND TAIL

It is at this point, before returning to the word of Merlin, that we can introduce a new symbolic application of the primal Dragons, the opening key to the entire visionary and prophetic sequence.

The rioting of the planetary order shows both an internal and external breakdown of established order; some of this astrological symbolism employs obvious opposites, direct inversions of the behaviour or attributes normally ascribed. In keeping with prophetic or apocalyptic visions in general we may expect to find Dragon symbolism in the visions of Merlin.

Astrologically, the Dragons are shown as the Lunar Nodes, or Dragon's Head and Tail. These nodes move backwards through the Zodiacal signs, and a period of eighteen years passes during a complete cycle of all the signs.

Traditionally the South Node, Dragon's Tail, is regarded as a negative influence, while the North Node, Dragon's Head, is positive. At one time the Nodes played a far greater role in astrology than they do today, though they are regarded as extremely important in some eastern astrological systems, where they are still linked with the dragons or energy streams of the human entity.

The Nodes are symbolically related to collective consciousness; and in this respect they are important to the analysis of the Red and White Dragons in the visions of Merlin.

North and South Nodes are exactly opposite one another in the horoscope; the North is exalted in Gemini, while the South is in Sagittarius.[5]

We might say, in old fashioned astrological terminology, that Merlin was born when the Dragon's Head was in Gemini, and the Dragon's tail in Sagittarius. In the individual seeking the insight exemplified by Merlin, applying the methods taught by

him inwardly, an analogous *re-birth* must be undertaken.
(Figure 6)

This train of concepts inevitably leads us back to the legend
of Merlin's conception, that he was born of a supernatural
father and a mortal mother. Furthermore, he is 'discovered' by
Vortigern through his argument with Dinabutius (the accusing
twin or brother of ancient myth, one half of Gemini) and then
he is catalysed and shot forth into prophetic consciousness by
the challenge of the false magicians and the aroused Dragons
(the action of Sagittarius). (See Chapter 5)

When Merlin is at the gates of the city (Kaermerdin) with his
comrade/brother/twin/accuser, he is situated at the Dragon's
Tail, the foot of the Hill. When he gains the prophetic insight,
he ascends to the Dragon's Head, from within the Hill itself up
to its Crown. And so the Tower may be completed, with the
Dragon or Dragons coiled around it.

The cycle of the Lunar nodes is a small reflection of the great
precession of the Equinoxes, and when we encounter the
Dragon symbolism in Merlin texts, we are probably dealing
with the remnant of an esoteric astrology that defined the
dynamics of spiritual energies and of cosmic evolution.

(91)   *The Gemini shall omit their usual embrace, and will
call the Urn (Aquarius) to the fountains./The Scales of Libra
shall hang awry, till Aries puts his crooked horns under
them./The tail of Scorpio shall produce lightning, and Cancer
quarrel with the Sun./Virgo shall mount upon the back of
Sagittarius, and darken her Virgin flowers.*

The images of disorder may be read in a number of ways, and
we must realize that the astrology of the early medieval period,
or of the earlier centuries from which this passage may be
derived, was a more directly magical system than that
employed today.

To come to grips with some of the potential polarities shown
by the astrological signs and planets, we must consider them as
both Magical Images (used for concentration, meditation and
invocation) and as astrological relationships in the intellectual
sense.

BIRTH OF MERLIN

IMAGES The Twins separate, and send the Water Carrier to the fountains. We may interpret this as the cessation of polarized (inner or outer) activity, such as consciousness or physical reaction (cause and effect), in which a third element is called from its usual role, and directed to the central source of all being. This theme recurs towards the close of the cosmic vision, and is reminiscent of the Three Fountains symbolism at the opening of the second chapter of *The Prophecies*.

ASTROLOGY We have exactly the same problem with the astrological sequence as with the broader panoply of *The Prophecies*; some of the material holds keys to an altered awareness, some of it does not. The main tone of the astrological passages is one of symbolic disruption, and this is more important to the author (Geoffrey and his source or sources) than a mathematical astrology or a contrived set of relationships.

The disruptive imagery is particularly potent when we consider the context of a medieval world-view. The geocentric astrological system was a prime model of divine order, and the images of its disruption were more imaginatively effective to a man or woman of the twelfth century than to a modern.

The riot of the Signs and Planets, with the subsequent sequence of primal dissolution for which it sets the tone, is not Christian. Apart from the traditional astrology, the images in the closing vision are a mixture of classical and native pagan lore. While we can observe a classical Greek or Roman literary source at work it is used as a veil for a recognizably British, and probably Welsh or Breton, pagan cosmology.

This symbolic osmosis, in which levels of shared consciousness permeate one another in an organic manner, applies to the astrology in a manner familiar to the meditator or practical magician, but less acceptable to the literary and historical intellect. Put simply, an esoteric astrology seems to exist 'behind' regular astrology.[6]

Esoteric astrology is not a secret or advanced teaching, but a mode of perception. It may be apprehended intellectually only by suggesting that it operates through hierarchies of psychic modelling, similar to those indicated in our Figure 1. If we were to remove astrology to a different or 'higher' mode of consciousness, yet retain it as astrology, we would perceive an esoteric astrological model.

This esoteric model is also the astrology of the very distant past, a psychic and prehistoric past in which the relationship between humankind and the stellar and planetary patterns was more potent and intimate than that of today. If the individual consciousness is opened to this relationship, esoteric astrology comes alive within the awareness and eventually permeates the psychic-body complex. It may occur as visions, contemplative states, or even as direct outer reactions in a highly ritualized or mythically charged sequence.

To appreciate this material on a practical level, we might attempt a series of dramatic enactments, in which a group of people take on the roles of the Signs, and perform a simple choreography of the movements described by Merlin.

This superficially child-like game is more than a mere psycho-drama or group interaction session; it is a ritualization of deep and powerful modes of consciousness rooted through time into the ground of being itself. Such a practical enactment is a valuable preparation for the individual catalysis, in which the process becomes internal and irrevocable. To demonstrate some of the applications of the imagery employed, we could imagine it in a hypothetical context, that of the ancient Mystery.

A candidate for initiation has spent many months or even years learning the astrological and mythical relationships between the Signs and Planets, and the meditative concepts have become an integral part of his or her understanding of shared reality. The candidate is utterly imbued with the powers and effects of this system, based upon a creation model of the four Primal Elements (Air, Fire, Water, Earth), and begins to grasp deep patterns of order, relationship, wholeness and integration.

The initiation ritual is a dramatic enactment, in which the candidate for the Mystery expects to enter into a new perception of truth, a new level of consciousness related to the great and beautiful patterns of the Elements, Signs and Planets. In a sacred cave, grove, or chamber, the initiation ceremony begins.

*Each of the ten or twelve actors in this ritual drama
performs not a further model of the Cosmic Order, but a
radically disruptive sequence, similar to that found at the
close of* The Prophecies. *Not a chaotic or frivolous disorder,
but one based upon a perception of reality encapsulated by
tradition and enlivened by individual experience and insight.*

*What effect would such an initiation ritual have upon the
candidate?*

With these suggestions in mind, we can return to the
sequence of Images suggested by *The Prophecies*:

1   GEMINI AND AQUARIUS: The Twins stand aside to
right and left, revealing the Water Carrier between them.
2   LIBRA AND ARIES: The Ram sets his Horns underneath
the Scales, setting right an imbalance that has developed
suddenly.
3   SCORPIO AND CANCER: The Scorpion emits lightning
from its tail, while the Crab fights with the Sun.
4   VIRGO AND SAGITTARIUS: The Virgin climbs upon
the back of Centaur, and by doing so loses her virginity.

If we consider each of these pairs of signs as an image,
visualized and meditated upon, they become not merely
contrived poetry for disorder, but complex and powerful
psychic and magical Keys.

A technical survey of the astrological relationships may
reveal mathematical relationships, and a modern astrologer
armed with a computer could produce a number of analogies
from the scenarios described by Merlin. In our present context,
we are confined to the basic mythical and magical roots of the
symbols concerned, and not with the fine points implied by
astrology in the modern sense. When we examine the roles of
Orion and the Pleiades in the following pages, we shall find
that some of the complex calculations of ancient star-lore have
permeated through into the imagery.

There is a difference, however, between observational stellar
magical lore, by which ancient temples were aligned, seasons
counted, actions such as sowing and reaping undertaken, and
specific magical practices were timed, and the intellectual
system used in modern astrology. In the modern system, the

psychic model is removed from observed patterns in the sky, or actual rising of stars and planets, and operates in a formalized dimension expressed by the circle of the birth chart. This method would have been regarded as bizarre by the ancients who linked their outer and inner worlds in the most intimate rhythmic ways, seeking to coalesce the movements of seasons, people, planets and stars into one unified dance.

The accuracy of modern astrology cannot be denied,[7] but it is no longer a magical and active system; it is passive and interpretative. During the twelfth century, astrology was composed of both the magical and the intellectual elements, and still relied strongly upon actual observation, combined with calculation and intuition.

(92) *The Chariot of the Moon shall disorder the Zodiac, and the Pleiades break forth into weeping./No offices of Janus shall return hereafter, but his gate being shut shall lie hid in the chinks of Ariadne./ (Giles)*

(92) *The Chariot of the Moon shall disturb the Zodiac, and the Pleiades shall burst into tears and lamentation./ None hereafter shall return to his wonted duty, but Ariadne shall lie hidden within the closed gateways of her sea-girt headland. (Evans)*

After the pairing of the Signs, we move into a new level of imagery, closer to the primal Elements.

There is a clear progression at work in the imagery; beginning with the line '*Root and branch will change places . . .*' we find the following order:

PLANETS Sun, Mercury, Mars, Venus. Mars, Mercury, Orion, Sun, Jupiter, Venus, Saturn. (In order of appearance in text. *Orion* is a constellation.)

HOUSES 'The Twelve Houses of the Stars shall lament the irregular excursions of their guests.'

SIGNS Gemini, Aquarius/Libra, Aries/ Scorpio, Cancer. Only six of the twelve are listed in the text.

CHARIOT OF THE MOON Luna was frequently depicted

driving horses and chariot through the heavens. We shall return to this image shortly.

THE PLEIADES   The Pleiades are examined below.

The units are moving from expression into elemental powers, from the Outward manifestation to the Inner reality. This may be shown in two diagrammatic forms (Figure 7). The first diagram is that of the geocentric system, in which the consciousness moves 'outwards' until, beyond the Signs, it reaches to the mysterious Stars. The second diagram is the inverse of this, and shows the psychic symbols dissolving into simpler units as the consciousness progresses inwardly towards Origination.

> (93)   *The seas shall rise up in the twinkling of an eye, and the dust of the Ancients be restored./The winds shall fight together with a dreadful blast, and their Sound shall reach to the Stars.*

In this last line of *The Prophecies*, we return to the basic Elements: WATER: 'the seas', EARTH: 'the dust of the Ancients', AIR: 'the winds', FIRE: 'the Stars'. The most obvious fiery symbol, the SUN, has already disappeared by this stage.

The progression from manifestation to inward and primary elemental states of being which include the origins of both matter and consciousness is a hallmark of the mystical experience, and of the magical traditions of transformation through psychic and spiritual interaction.

Merlin is describing a cosmic cataclysm, the disordering of our solar system (be it geocentric or heliocentric), but he is also revealing the inner transformation that occurs within the human consciousness. Ultimately the two are the same.

During the 'passing within', the movement of awareness through Planets, Houses, Signs and Elements, certain indicators are met.

Both Orion and the Pleiades play an obscure but important role in esoteric traditions, particularly those connected with ritual magical traditions and with alchemy.

To come to a clear understanding of these indicators, we

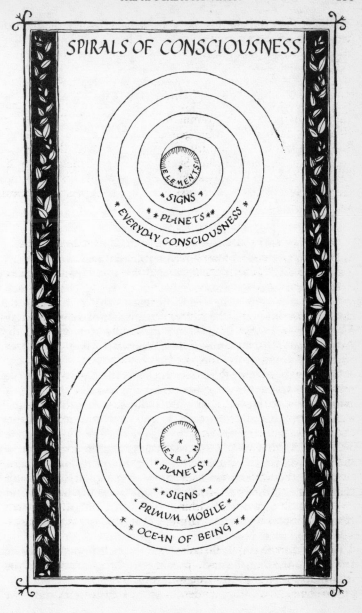

should consider them not only as isolated symbolic entities within the psyche and within human cultural development, but in their specific relationship to one another within Merlin's vision, and the order in which they appear.

It is the order of constituent symbols that reveals a pattern to the vision, and which suggests that we are not encountering a poetic contrivance of disorder, written for dramatic effect (though this aim does have some influence upon Geoffrey's re-working of *The Prophecies*).

After we have passed through the Planets, Houses and Signs, but before we come to the Elements, we encounter the Chariot of the Moon, suggestively linked to the Pleiades.

THE CHARIOT OF THE MOON

The Moon Goddess is often given a role of passivity in modern interpretation, but to the ancients she was a great and often terrifying power. Her association with horses reaches far back to primitive fertility beliefs, and in Britain she is linked to the native goddess Epona, the Mare. A pediment of approximately the first century AD in the temple of Sulis-Minerva at Bath, shows Luna with her long whip. The horse is a symbol of power in motion.

Luna's chariot moves rapidly through the Signs, as can be seen by observing her directly in the night and day skies. She is associated with the tides, not only the great rhythms of the seas, but the equally unavoidable ebb and flow of the inner tides. These tides affect us each individually, and also operate on vast collective areas of consciousness and life experience.

The Moon is associated with the life and death polarities of all living beings, expressed through the Signs, Houses and Planets. She is the great goddess of the ancient religions, and for her Chariot to 'disturb the Zodiac', as Merlin says, is a very great disruption of rhythm and creation.

We could imagine a physical situation, in which the satellite that represents the inner Moon detaches itself from the regular orbit about the planet Earth. This has been suggested by science as a disaster of the far distant future, in which the physical Moon might fall into the Earth. More suggestively, this is a disruption of the most fundamental rhythms of consciousness, of the polarities of being itself. While the Sun represents a central awareness, the Moon represents the source and foundation of that awareness, and its almost indissoluble ties to all other life forms. Once again, we are confronted with that catalytic sequence in which consciousness has to be broken down to reach into its energetic sources.

The visions of Merlin do not offer an obvious reconstitution to follow the cataclysm, for they show both individual and cosmic cycles, extending to the ultimate end or breakdown. Other parts of the *History*, however, and the *Vita Merlini* in particular, clearly suggest traditional methods of re-creation, of world-making, both cosmically and in terms of human awareness.

THE PLEIADES AND ORION

Two constellations are specifically mentioned by Merlin, inserted into the planetary and astrological references. They seem at first to be oddities, out of keeping with the general simple system that develops and leads us to the vision of dissolution. Orion occurs near the opening of the sequence, and the Pleiades towards the conclusion.

Once again, we have a choice: did Merlin/Geoffrey include these references merely for poetic effect, or to give the text authority through classical allusion, or are we encountering the veiled remnant of a coherent and meaningful set of symbols? If the images were merely chosen at random, we shall find that the author hit upon some remarkably pertinent material by accident.

As we have suggested in the speculations upon Merlin's own horoscope and his connection with the Lunar Nodes, symbolized by a Dragon, our text draws upon some very complex and ancient star-lore. Such lore is not merely a crude forerunner of modern astrology, but involves symbolic and seasonal patterns fundamental to human life activity. Medieval astrology included methods and interpretations that seem excessive to the modern astrologer, yet much of this fluid and literal interpretation was drawn from the widespread mythical and magical traditions which permeated the society of the period.

When we examine the star-lore in Merlin's final vision, we are dealing with a fusion of three streams of imagery: ancient British seasonal and mythical star-lore, Greek astrology and related classical myths, and the basic elemental system of geocentrism followed during the medieval period. To the modern reader the differences may seem academic or even trifling, but the conceptual models involved vary in several important respects.

1   *Primal star-lore* is related to observation and rhythm, and is essentially a practical system. The intellectual model of the Elements, Qualities, Signs, Planets and so forth, is not necessary in this primal lore, though obviously it underpins it and helps to analyse it. Primal star lore is closely attuned to deep rhythms within the individual psyche, related in turn to the environment, and again related to the patterns of the stars through the year. It is not an intellectual system; it is a poetic one.

Although we have suggested that the primal lore is 'ancient British', its primacy is shared by all races, and is not a property of any one people. The British element suggested comes from Geoffrey's use of native oral tradition, which contained many wisdom tales and allusions to magical and astrological lore. With the exception of certain clearly British (Welsh or Breton) names, much of the material in the *History* is given a classical allusion; the mythical beings or their functions are cloaked in Greek or Roman names. This general practice, well established long before the medieval period, merely follows the Roman usage of calling native symbols, deities, powers and places by Latinized substitution names, and leads us to the Greek mythical and astrological element in the Merlin text.

2   *The primal myths* are shared myths, and much of the British lore is held in common with classical Greek lore. To Geoffrey this was a proof of the origin of the house of Brutus, the eponymous founder of Britain. In his curious poetical manner, Geoffrey has been proved correct time and time again, providing we take his *History* as being traditional rather than literal; a history in which persons, places and events are defined by their function of mythic value rather than by accurate cross reference. To the occultist or student of obscure esoteric lore,

Geoffrey's flight of Brutus is a repetition of the ancient flight from Atlantis, which we first find in Greek traditions, said to be drawn from Egyptian sources.

In this confused but suggestive context, it is interesting to note that there are some specific references to Britain in Greek mythology as the Hyperborean lands (i.e. those beyond the North Wind), true home of Apollo.[8]

Geoffrey, therefore, cloaks his star-lore in Greek mythological terminology, and in Greek astrological references. To come to grips with this literary and quite normal substitution, for the medieval scholar was imbued with certain aspects of classical symbolism, we must repeatedly consider the *function* of the being, star, or constellation described. It is through this attitude that we make the primal connections necessary to bring the magic of the Prophecies alive.

3 *The geocentric system* provides the map for the stages of the cosmic vision, and is basically the map still employed by astrologers today, though geocentrism is no longer accepted as a physical model of the Universe. One of the most commonplace errors in judging the geocentric system is to assume that it is invalid because disproven. As a conceptual model relating to consciousness and the human situation, the geocentric and Elemental system is an excellent analogy. It also provides the starting point for a sequence for inner realizations, by which the consciousness apprehends models of reality which are at the foundation of our group-world.

An excellent description of the traditional four-fold system is given by Geoffrey himself in the *Vita Merlini*, and although this world system is related to the classical authorities of his day, Geoffrey is likely to be drawing upon a wisdom poem from oral tradition. (See Appendix I)

From such a complex but harmonically related series of possible sources, we can proceed to the detailed examination of Orion and the Pleiades, and the reasons for their specific inclusion by Merlin in his catalogue of the breakdown of the geocentric solar system and the return of the Earth to its primal Elements.

ORION

'And Iron Orion shall unsheathe his sword . . .' (89)

Orion is the titanic hunter figure found in myths worldwide. In astrology or astronomy, Orion is the southern figure of four cardinal points: The Bear in the North, Orion the South, and the Pleiades rising in the East and setting in the West. As we shall shortly discover, Orion and the Pleiades have an especial relationship; while in British or Celtic lore, the Bear is a symbol of King Arthur.

Simply by identifying Orion, we are plunged into primal star-lore, where the observations used by travellers on land and sea were not only indicators of the seasons for journeying, but were also the signposts for an inner transition, in which the four directions become magical dimensions of consciousness.

We should remember that to our ancestors the inner and outer worlds were intimately related, and that there really was very little difference between the two states of being. By developing our rational sciences, we have widened the separation between the inner and outer dimensions, both in our consciousness and its application, and (according to esoteric sources) as a result of our nucleur experiments, which are said to have torn a rift between states of existence or worlds that were normally in relationship to one another. The nuclear explosion, therefore, becomes the epitomized physical expression of the ancient myth of the Fall of Lucifer.

In native mythology, Orion is similar to a number of figures, particularly those gigantic and potent beings like the Irish Dagda,[9] or the later Wayland Smith, himself a Saxon derivative of an earlier god of Fire and metal working.[10] His appearance at the opening of Merlin's final vision, is as a primal destructive figure, the Hunter of the Gods. Although the textual reference is brief, there is considerable evidence to support this theory.

In Egyptian astronomical/astrological symbolism, Orion, known as Sahu, leads a stellar hunt. He slays and consumes great and lesser gods, and men.[11] He is similar, therefore, to the Celtic ruler of the Wild Hunt, Lord of the Animals, Ruler of the UnderWorld. This is Orion's dark potent frightening aspect. A Biblical variant of this theme may have been known to

Geoffrey, in the form of the giant Nimrod, rebellious against Jehovah, and so cast into the sky for punishment. Nimrod was the builder of the Tower of Babel.[12] 'And Cush begat Nimrod; he began to be a mighty one on the earth. . . . wherefore it is said, Like Nimrod, a mighty hunter before the Lord.' (Genesis 10,9-10.)

Orion is also identified with the Sun, and has a particular influence upon the seas.[13] Although his solar attributes show a brighter side, our attention is drawn to the marine and stormy qualities of Orion's symbolism, by the line: 'The watery Sun shall torment the clouds . . .' This dire influence clearly derives from various classical sources, where the destructive effect of Orion upon the seas was repeatedly stated. To sail after the rising of Orion, while the Giant was visible in the sky, was to invite disaster.

Although we may ascribe this subtlety to Geoffrey of Monmouth's ability to show off his classical knowledge, it nevertheless represents a primal star- and weather-lore, related to dissolution and death. The medieval scholar, listener, and even the ordinary sailor, would have understood the baleful effect of Orion heaving his gigantic shoulders over the horizon.

The classical sources available to Geoffrey might have included Hesiod, Vergil, Horace, and Pliny, all of whom refer to Orion in terms such as 'Nautis infestus', 'horridus sideribus' and similar epithets which leave us in no doubt as to the true identity of 'the watery sun' seen by Merlin.

In Greek mythology and astrology, various legends are attached to Orion in his role as Hunter. Homer depicts Orion in the Underworld, where Odysseus sees him brandishing a club of solid copper, unbroken and unbreakable. It is Homer, also, who describes the Bear watching Orion from the North, to ensure that the Hunter will not attack him.

Orion is connected also to the Moon, in the legend of the trick whereby Diana, the hunting Goddess of the Moon, shot her lover (Orion) while he swam far out to sea. The plot was originated by Apollo, jealous of his sister's attentions to a primal and Titanic power. Once again, we find Orion connected to the sea, and at the close of Merlin's vision a goddess closes the doors of creation, which become hidden in an enveloping cloud, while the seas rise up.

Other legends show the relationship between Orion and Scorpio, for when the Scorpion rises, Orion sets, and so the Hunter is fleeing from the venomous creature that pursues him. Most important, in our present context, is Orion's relationship to the Pleiades.

THE PLEIADES

The Pleiades are important, not only through the famous descriptions and allusions found in early writings, myths and legends, all derived from their role of marking time and seasons, but also through their appearance in esoteric wisdom traditions.[14] While the primal star-lore of the Pleiades is outwardly related to the passage of the seasons, the inner teaching suggests that they are also the indicators of cosmic phases. Quite how they act is uncertain in this esoteric context, but we shall see that the Pleiades were of great ritual and observational importance to the ancients in the cycle of annual life; it is likely that this significance was extended harmonically to the belief that they had a similar role in the 'year' of the solar system.

In magical teachings, the Pleiades are said to be the stellar matrix for the seven Planets of the solar system, though materially this cannot be the case as the septenary pattern is idealized, derived from the viewpoint of an observer on Earth. Here we have the geocentric system once again, not outdated and disproven through advance of science, but applied as a model of relationships between inner awareness and outer observation. The precession of the equinox, the great cycle (of which the Lunar cycle mentioned above is a reflection), is also called 'the Great Year of the Pleiades', and lasts approximately 25,900 years. It is from this astronomical/astrological observation made in the distant past that esoteric teachings linked to the Pleiades are derived.[15]

Among the many attributes of the Pleiades, we should note that their Egyptian connection was with Neith, the Shuttle or Weaving goddess. The Greeks identified this power with Athena, and the Romans with Minerva. At the close of Merlin's vision, the great goddess appears as Ariadne, another image connected with weaving, or with the Spider. This skein of connections is very apt in the context of the cycle of precession, the Great Year of the Pleiades, for the shape of an astrological map is very similar to the shape of a spider's web.[16]

So important were the Seven Sisters to the Greeks, that the temples of Athena were aligned to their rising, while those of Bacchus and Asclepius are known to be aligned to their setting. The mysterious connection between the Pleiades and the cosmic cycle is also found in South America and Mexico. The plunderer Cortez heard a native tradition in the sixteenth century of these stars associated with the destruction of the world.[17]

Of particular relevance in the Merlin symbology, is the use of the Pleiades as markers of the two great turning points of the Seasons. In Celtic practice, perpetuated by folk customs well into the nineteenth and twentieth centuries, the rising of the Pleiades in November marked the festival of the blessed ancestors. Today this is known as Samhain, All Hallows, or Hallowe'en, when the dead draw close to the living, and the gates between the worlds are opened. All fires were extinguished at this time, a practice known worldwide, and the spirits of the dead were supposed to pass into the Otherworld. At the culmination of the Pleiades, a fresh magical fire was lit ritually, and from this flames carried far and wide. The fanciful ceremonies still found in parts of Britain today, involving bonfires, flaming barrels and similar practices, are all echoes of this Druidic rite. Even the ritualized burning of Guy Fawkes is merely a later commemorative variant of the fire festival associated with the Pleiades.

The attempt to blow up the King on 5 November 1605 has some clear symbolic connections with the destructive role of the Pleiades mentioned above, as markers of the cosmic clock of order, and harbingers of great disaster. Little wonder that widespread folk custom incorporated the Gunpowder Plot into its fabric intuitively.

The May festival of Beltane was also marked by the Pleiades. It is the balancing opposite of the festival of the dead, and occurs at the mid-point of a year running from November to November. The May rituals, still perpetuated today in folk ceremonies such as the 'Obby 'Oss of the English West Country, and various fire lighting customs in Scotland and

Brittany, were a celebration of new life. Beli or Bel, from whom the word Beltane derives, was a Celtic god of Light.

The old Beltane ceremonies were used to purify and rejoice through fire, and involved dances in which the celebrants leapt through the flames of ritually kindled bonfires.

The Pleiades, therefore, by their movement, rising and setting, were employed as markers of the seasons, and were particularly associated with the powers of life and death. Their weeping at the close of Merlin's vision is particularly apt, for this appearance is the close of the great year or cycle of the solar system, the dissolution of our reality.

In Greek mythology, we find the Pleiades pursued by the lustful Orion, a myth connected to their relative positions. Orion, therefore, the potent Hunter, and the Pleiades, the Seven Stars of Life and Death, act out the great drama of life, desire, and death, represented in Merlin's vision by the Three Streams (see verse 42).

The relationship between Orion and the Pleiades may be seen as that of Energy and Qualities of expression. Orion is tremendous personification of raw power, while the Pleiades are the refining qualities through which this power is expressed. We can detect an analogy between these stellar symbols, and the relationship between the Sun (personified by ancient variants of Orion) and the Seven Planets (often connected with the septenary of the Pleiades). The Seven were Maia, the mother of Mercury, Taygeta, Celaeon, Asterope, Alcyone, Electra, and Merope. Each of these has mythological inter-connections which reveal her to be a focus or matrix for qualities of consciousness in expression. (see Figure 8).

The Pleiades, therefore, are the physical stellar expression of a female septenary, seven essential inner qualities that define the sequence of life and death.

We might suggest that while the Seven Planets are the obvious indicators of these qualities within the individual birth chart, the Pleiades are a higher octave or harmonic of these qualities, and have a collective application.

As the images move towards simple units, they become more powerful, more primal. From the Seven Sisters, Merlin carries our imagination on to the Doorkeeper, and the weaver goddess, Ariadne.

ORION & THE PLEIADES

CHAPTER 10
Ariadne closes the Gate

'No offices of Janus shall return hereafter, but the gate being
shut shall lie hid in the chinks of Ariadne.' Giles (92)
'None hereafter shall return to his wonted duty, but Ariadne
shall lie hidden within the closed gateways of her sea-girt
headland.' Evans
'None of these shall return to the duty expected of it.
Ariadne will shut its door and be hidden within the enclosing
cloudbanks.' Thorpe

The three variant translations quoted above all contain the
same basic elements:
  (a) Change of office, role, or duty.
  (b) A closed gateway.
  (c) Sea or clouds.
  (d) Ariadne.

  (a) *The change of office* refers to the disorder of the cosmic
symbols, discussed above. JANUS is the Doorkeeper, a god
who looks two ways, either to the old and new year, or both
inward and outward. He guards the gateway between the
dimensions, the human world and the Otherworld, and a lesser
harmonic of Janus exists within each personality as that which
closes the doorways to deeper levels of consciousness and
guards the individual from energies that he or she is not able or
not willing to bear.[1]
  (b) *From the Gatekeeper*, we come to the Gate itself. At the
closing of the ordered system, the dissolution of the geocentric
or heliocentric system, the originative life-power retires behind
a closed door. This door is the barrier that features in many
mystical visions or dreams; in formal worship sites it is the rail
before the altar, while in magical temples it is the Black and
White Pillars of alternating polarity in power.

The Gate or Door is a necessary barrier between our perceiving consciousness and reality; to pass beyond it is to court death.

(c) *The encompassing clouds* or seas are the Veil which is found before the face of Divinity; in this case it is the Goddess, and her presence is shrouded not out of sense of illusion, but as a protecting filter for the mystic or seer who seeks to find Truth direct.

There are three stages of approach defined within this vison: the Gatekeeper or Guardian; the Closed Door; the Veil of Clouds.

While the Gatekeeper is personified by certain innerworld beings with specific role in the Mysteries, such as Janus, Hercules, the Gnostic Christ, and many others, he is also that dark power of restraint that must be confronted to gain spiritual illumination. He has two heads not only because he looks within and without, but because of this twofold nature inherent in his function as Guardian and Initiator.

Robert Graves published a significant commentary upon this sequence in his *White Goddess*: 'What I take for a reference to Llyr (the British Sea-God) as Janus occurs in the closing paragraph of Merlin's prophecy to the heathen King Vortigern and his Druids, recorded by Geoffrey of Monmouth: *After this Janus shall never have priests again. His door will be shut up and remain concealed in Ariadne's crannies.* In other words, the ancient Druidic religion based on the oak-cult will be swept away by Christianity and the door – the god Llyr – will languish forgotten in the Castle or Arianrhod, the *Corona Borealis*.'[2]

Janus is also mentioned by Geoffrey in the *History* proper, where Cordelia buries her father Leir (later to become famous as Shakespeare's King Lear) under the ground in a vault dedicated to Janus. All the workmen used to gather in this vault to celebrate the beginning of each year of labour. (*Historia*, II, 14.)

Although Graves uses the reference to forward his calendrical argument, and we employ it here in a more metaphysical or even psychological role, it is clear in either case that a god or power of Doorkeeping was important, if not central, in the practices of our ancestors.

This is supported by the symbolism of orthodox religion and of magic throughout the world, thus defining the Doorkeeper or Guardian as a property of human consciousness, and as an Archetype (in the original sense of the word) defining a presentation of the Divine or the Unknown in a form that generates reaction and response.

In Celtic tradition, the Gatekeeper was a person of special importance, who had the right to bar entry to anyone; this magical right was followed in daily life, and features in the tales of the court of King Arthur, and in the Irish hero tales. In formalized magical lodge practice, the Doorkeeper may bar admission to any member or supplicant, even today. The ritualized admission sequence carried out annually by the English Parliament is likely to be a corrupt derivation of such magical practices, though it has been rationalized as a statement of parliamentary authority over the Crown.[3]

From the Guardian or Gatekeeper, we come to the closed Door. In magical initiation or mystical insight, whoever passes the Guardian may have the door opened. After the contest of Guardianship, the Door represents the next barrier. It is a less awesome task than the Two Headed Keeper, but presents a subtle challenge, for a greater terror lies beyond it than that which was conquered to open it.

In Merlin's vision, we again experience a multiple meaning, for the closed door is either the withdrawal of originative energy at the end of a creative period, or the end of the life of the Solar system, or it is a guide to an initiatory realization.

There are many secrets of Door-opening: passwords, riddles, magical incantations, meditative techniques. Britain is called the Island of the Strong Door in traditional legend; one method of door-opening is found in the arousal of the Dragons. Other methods are also known from tradition, including an esoteric teaching whereby Arthur, or even Merlin himself, exist inwardly as doorkeepers and door-openers for those that dare to approach them. The magical door of Britain is situated in the north of the Magical Circle, and therefore marked with the symbol of the Bear.

Behind the Door, there is Cloud. This is the last Veil or barrier before the face of the Goddess, who is the originator of creation itself. While the Guardian may be challenged, and the

Door may be opened, none may penetrate the Veil and live. This ancient wisdom teaching refers to physical death, but may also indicate the secrets of the 'living death' of spiritual enlightenment.

As symbolized by the catalysis of Merlin, to see the Goddess, to know Reality, is to be destroyed. In magical development, however, this does not necessarily imply a mere physical death. The death is a death of false personality, in which many layers of illusory self-image are stripped away (the riot of the Signs) leaving the primal energy shining in its glory.

Ancient cultures termed their initiates the 'living dead', not out of any puerile goulish fantasy, but because such men and women had been reborn into a reality so different from that of the group-world, that they were no longer bound to it. They had, in effect, seen the sights of death in the Otherworld while still living as physical human beings. In the classical Mysteries this experience is described as the Sun at Midnight.[4]

(d) *Ariadne* The goddess hides behind her veil of clouds. It is remarkable that there is no Christian influence whatsoever in this last phase of Merlin's vision. This magical and pagan symbolism is firm evidence of the traditional nature of the poetry, preserved by word of mouth through its inherent sanctity. It is clear that Geoffrey could, for example, have drawn on Apocalyptic material from the Bible, but the progression of symbols has a clear integrity, a continuity which may also be traced in the earlier parts of *The Prophecies*.

We have already found that Ariadne was identified with the Welsh goddess Arianrhod by Graves, writing in 1944. There is a strange and powerful interconnection of symbols in *The Prophecies*, and ultimately they all lead to this mysterious female power.

The Pleiades were identified by the ancients with a goddess of weaving, and also marked the extremes of the cycle of the year. The poetical '13th Sign' of the Zodiac is of course the weaving goddess, sometimes shown as a Spider; this is Ariadne. In Greek myth, Ariadne is connected with the hero Theseus. He finds his way through a complex maze, the Labyrinth, in which he slays the bull-headed Minotaur. Ariadne provides him with a thread, by which he can find his way out again.[5] Like Minerva or Athena with whom the Egyptian weaver-goddess

Nieth was identified, Ariadne is a goddess who helps heroes.

We may see in this myth a sequence very similar to that offered by Merlin; the Labyrinth is the complex pattern of personal or geocentric Zodiac. The Minotaur is the Guardian who must be encountered before penetrating the mysteries, while Ariadne is not merely a princess waiting to be saved, she is the originator and judge of the entire venture.[6]

Curiously we find this motif repeated in the story of Henry II and Fair Rosamund. This Rose of the World was kept hidden in the centre of a labyrinth at Woodstock, where the King would visit her in secret. Unfortunately the jealous Queen followed a silken thread attached to the King's spur, and so found and later poisoned his mistress. This is no idle tale, but based upon historical fact. The symbolic elements of silken thread and maze have become attached to a real situation; and Rosamund was treated with great reverence by the poor after her death, who worshipped her as a saint. Why should a King's mistress be revered by the common people? Probably through some traditional pagan practice or custom associated with a native goddess, and further accumulated by the attachment of the silken-thread motif in popular re-tellings of the tale.[7]

In the traditional ballad 'Giles Collins', we meet a maiden who is 'sewing a silver seam'. She commands the life and death of the hero of the ballad; she is derived from the same ancient goddess who wove the thread of destiny for those brave enough to follow it.[8]

Theseus was also associated with a raid upon the Under-World, to capture its queen, Persephone. He failed in this, however, as he had to be aided by the great hero Hercules. The theme of the raid upon the mysterious UnderWorld runs through Celtic legends, and even King Arthur is said to have made such a heroic venture.[9]

While we can make no literary historical direct connection it is most likely that the integrity of the Merlin vision to oral wisdom teachings and poems implies that Ariadne is a native goddess. We have evidence from British traditions that such a weaving goddess existed, and it is reasonable to name her as Arianrhod, the Goddess of the Silver Wheel.

In the 'Corpus Christi Carol', a merging of pagan and esoteric Christian lore, we find a dying knight attended by a hound and a maiden who sews with silver thread. These oral sources, such as 'Giles Collins' and 'Corpus Christi', are particularly important, as they have not undergone tampering or editing, being preserved solely in the common imagination for many centuries.[10]

This final vision, of the goddess who holds the central thread of creation and destruction within a secret chamber, carries us beyond anthropomorphic symbolism.

The goddess Ariadne is the last image, or perhaps we might say the first person, before the primal Elements. Merlin's prophetic ferment carries us even beyond the Goddess; on this last stage of the journey, we reach deep within ourselves, to find levels of energy and consciousness united with the rhythm of the life of the solar system, a life in which we have an integral part.

AFTER THE GODDESS

The seas shall rise up in the twinkling of an eye, and the dust of the Ancients be restored. (93)

After the reference to the weaver goddess, who holds the threads of destiny and manifestation together, we find one of the typical inversion phrases which run through the text. In this phrase, however, the content is identical to inner experience and esoteric teaching drawn from a western tradition.

To reach the chinks or crannies of Ariadne, we have to pass within, but we also pass beneath. The greatest mysteries are hidden within the Earth, and in many schools of enlightenment a journey underground is featured as an essential experience.

During such journeys, the individual gains contact with his or her ancestors; this is the property of the collective consciousness, and not mere spiritualism. It relies as much upon biological 'memory' as it does upon magical technique.

The Greeks, Romans, Celts, and later peoples of Europe were all intimately involved in ancestor cults; the 'blessed dead' were not a sentimental orthodox platitude but a living power in the lives of our forebears. Dedication to this concept ranged from intense and complex ancient rituals to customs of honour which are still carried out in various forms today.

Put simply, the dead have moved from this world to another; but we partake of their nature through our blood ties, shared cultures, and inherent communal consciousness. Such would be a modern re-statement of the ancient beliefs, up to a certain point. The pagan cultures went beyond this, and asserted that the ancestral spirits might be contacted, might be appeased if angry, and might also confer blessing and wisdom to the living. A major part of the temple practices and the instruction of the Mysteries was concerned with the activities of the realm of the dead.

In modern magical initiation (if it is of any genuine value) the student is prepared for a mode of consciousness in which he or she gains access to a vast pool of consciousness through time, in which the voices of many ancestors are clearly heard, and their memories clearly depicted. This state is not similar in any way to the so-called 'spirit messages' of mediums, as it occurs at a far deeper level of consciousness, and has many properties in common with the 'collective unconscious' of some schools of materialist psychology.

If one pushes this consciousness inward and backward in time, it can theoretically lead to very early ancestral images. Generation of this arousal is part of the cathartic training of western techniques of enlightenment.

We find a similar sequence of progression in the old magical ballad of 'Thomas Rhymer'; a man meets a mysterious Faery Queen, she takes him Underground, he hears the roaring of the sea and wades through rivers of blood and water, he then sees wonders, and finally returns to the human world after seven years. As a result of this experience, he becomes a bard and a seer.[11]

While this may sound like a fantastical tale, Thomas Rhymer was a historical person, living not long after Geoffrey of Monmouth. Thomas wrote a number of prophecies in vernacular verse, many of which have clearly come true. Like Merlin, he concentrated upon national insight, for Thomas's verses deal with the history of Scotland. There are striking similarities between the lore of Merlin and that of Thomas and the Faery Queen; both represent a British or Celtic tradition of enlightenment through catalysis, under the blessing of a female power.

The cloudbanks, sea, and dust of the ancients are all the

Veil. This collective cloud of past knowledge, even down to a cellular level if we were able to reach so far, makes the Veil within human awareness. When we first approach the Veil, it acts as a protecting cloud; when its contents are activated, they come alive through the mediation of the powers of the Goddess (Ariadne). After an encounter with her, or knowledge of her reality, we can experience the Veil as a numinous cloud of potential surrounding the primal source of Reality. This passing in and out of the Veil during transformation is a human analogue of the greater Veil of Stars which hides and yet reveals the face of divinity in the Universe.

Before moving to the last line of *The Prophecies*, we should repeat the order of metaphysical events encapsulated in the progress of the Final Vision.

1	Root and Branch change places.	The UnderWorld Tree.
2	The Planets are disturbed and Orion appears. Saturn reaps death among mankind.	Titanic powers of catalysis commence action.
3	The Houses of the Zodiac lament.	The ferment moves inward.
4	The Signs are disrupted.	Cosmic order is realigned.
5	The Chariot of the Moon acts as an agent of disorder.	Primal tides move in new ways.
6	The Pleiades weep.	The delimiting consciousness of the Great Year breaks down.
7	The Doorkeeper closes the Door (or guards its closure).	The innermost portal of reality is found but remains shut.
8	The Weaver Goddess is named, surrounded by clouds.	The veil before Reality is perceived by opening the Door.
9	The Seas and the Ancestors arise.	Within the veil is the shared consciousness of all past life.
10	The winds fight together and their sound reaches the stars.	The Four Primal Winds collide, and the solar system or earth system is dissolved.

THE FINAL DISSOLUTION

*The winds shall fight together with a dreadful blast, and
their Sound shall reach the Stars.*

The reference here is to the Four Winds, or four Elements of
The Wise. To the medieval scholar a phrase such as 'the winds'
is not a vague generalization such as we might use today; the
world-view of Geoffrey's period was based upon geocentric and
classical models in which the Four Winds played an important
part.

If we look at the Creation poem included in the *Vita Merlini*
(see Appendix I) the pattern of this model of creation is clear.
The winds are derived from, and metaphysically identical to,
the Four Elements of Air, Fire, Water, Earth, and to the
Fourfold Originative model emitted by the source of all Being.
The Elements fighting together is the final disorder; the door
has closed, the Goddess has withdrawn her controlling power
into the deep, and the primal powers collide and annihilate one
another.

The imagery is not only poetic, but also very precise. It
depicts the destruction of the solar system, and this event is so
powerful that the distant stars hear its sound. While the
medieval mind accepts this imagery as the breakdown of the
four-fold conceptual model and the geocentric pattern, it is an
accurate description to the modern intellect of the energies that
radiate across the depths of space. Modern astronomers can
'hear' the blasts emitted by stars that no longer exist; their
death conflict reaches us long after the event itself has occurred.
To our equipment, the universe is full of such sounds, emitting
across a wide spectrum of energies. Merlin's vision is still
accurate, even to the modern astronomer and physicist.

If we consider this last image in the terms of the psyche and
spiritual progression within any individual, it suggests that
mysterious and final stage of enlightenment in which the
consciousness loses its modes of polarity (the Four Winds) and
merges with the Unknown.

In eastern systems this is usually depicted as a passive and
calm process; the western symbolism, however, sees it as a
dramatic and even explosive final enlightenment. If the attuning

spirit withdraws, a vacuum is left, in which the Elements collide and neutralize one another. This terrifying nature of spiritual power is found in religious imagery, particularly that of the Old Testament.

The much discussed vision of Ezekiel has some similarities to the Merlin sequence, though placed in a patriarchal context. The prophet Enoch walked with God 'and was not'; other prophets were taken up to Heaven in tongues of Fire; the resurrected body of Jesus was of an order of reality previously unknown.

We should not see these religious parallels as 'authorities', but simply as examples of similar conceptual models, in which potent spiritual energies alter the outer reality in a very real and dynamic manner.

If we extend the comparison to its extreme, we might imagine that the physical body of the seer or individual undergoing the catalytic changes of enlightenment suddenly disappears; the resulting vacuum causes an implosion. Ridiculous as this sounds, there are continuing traditions of people who disappear physically into the Otherworld, and belief in this oddity is still found today. Some, such as Thomas Rhymer, return after a period of outer time; others, like the Reverend Robert Kirk, are still missing. This is not only a poetical device, but a deep-rooted motif suggestive of our intuitions of the nature of Reality.

In western techniques for attaining spiritual enlightenment, the self-image is destroyed. While eastern methods are often cited as being calm and contemplative in this respect, many of the ancient religions are allied to chthonic foundations, in which the illusory self is torn apart or eaten by fearsome entities. A similar method is employed in the western initiations, but it should be emphasized that there is a symbolic language and training system allied to techniques of inner realization, and that these essential preparatory stages enable the student to undergo the catalysis with a certain amount of foreknowledge.

The blast of the Four Winds is that shocking moment of inner perception, when the individual looks within, and truly knows that he or she *does not exist*.

AFTER THE END

We have followed Ariadne's thread through the complexities of Merlin's final Vision. It has led us to the Stars, and back into our physical bodies, even though these may mysteriously disappear! The solar system has vanished, and the Gates of Creation are shut. Life as we know it has ended; not all life, but our solar life, our physical life. If this cosmic vision has an analogy for spiritual enlightenment, and if it can be applied as a method of attaining wisdom, what happens next? It would be too easy to offer the type of spiritualized meaningless platitudes that feature regularly in books or classes on meditation, or in formal religion. Merlin's Vision is not of this sort; it offers perception of Truth, even to the extent of self-annihilation beyond the experience of the Goddess.

Traditionally, the initiate who gains the experience of primal consciousness has three choices. He or she may freely choose any one of the three if inner freedom (the dissolution of the Planets and Signs of the personal birth patterns) has been achieved. If this freedom has not been fully realized, the personal Chart will re-form after the primal Vision, though usually in a radically changed manner.

Merlin pushes the imagery and the magical transformations to their ultimate end, the dissolution. What are the three choices offered by esoteric teaching? In the ballad of Thomas Rhymer, the Faery Queen shows Thomas three roads: the narrow road of thorns and briars, the broad road between the lilies, and the green road to Elfland. These are one expression of the Threefold Choice, filtered through folk tradition.

The choices at the moment of dissolution are:

1 To merge with the Unknown.
2 To traverse the dimensions and enter another world.
3 To return to the outer world to help humanity.

This Threefold Choice brings us back to the Three Achievers of The Grail discussed in our first chapter.

Each of these three has a counterpart in the traditions relating to Faeryland:

1 Galahad: Merlin

2   Perceval: Thomas Rhymer
3   Bors: Robert Kirk

These counterparts should not be taken literally; they represent categories.

The first category includes a transformation that reaches right through to the physical body, creating the paradox of the physical translation into spiritual dimensions. In mystical experience, it is shown as utter unity with the Divine. In Galahad we find this symbolized by the pure Christian knight, a model of Christ on Earth, but his initiation of the Grail derives from pagan mysteries of regeneration.

In Merlin we find the Prophet of the Land, one who has penetrated so deeply into the mysteries of the Earth that he emerges in the Stars. This concept is found in the relationship between the Pleiades and Orion, and the Seven Planets and the Sun, which has been discussed in an earlier chapter. The traditional astrological symbols are found within the individual; the stellar analogues are found, metaphysically, within the Earth.

The second category is that of consciousness reaching into other dimensions, into which the traveller or initiate passes to fulfil a specific role. In the case of Perceval, this is to act as the ruler or king within the Grail Castle; he is the type of mediator known in modern esoteric terminology as an 'inner plane master'. More specifically, he acts as a priest and king of the Mysteries of the Grail, and his image mediates their power to the consciousness of the aspirant seeking enlightenment.

In Thomas Rhymer, we find one who has travelled into the UnderWorld, and entered the castle of the Faery Queen. He becomes her consort, and is gifted with poetry and seership. These are the means by which he mediates his consciousness, his relationship to the primal inner power, back to the aspirant. Unlike Merlin he does not disappear from contact into the depths of Creation, but passes to and fro as an active mediator.

The third category is that of spiritual illumination in service to humanity. Bors chose to sacrifice his inner freedom, and to return to the outer world to testify to the presence of the Grail. He represents a pattern of 'voluntary incarnation' in which service to humanity is known to be the highest devotion.

In Robert Kirk we find a Christian priest, but one who chose to reveal the 'secrets' of the Second Sight and the Otherworld; in folk tradition he is said to live on in close relationship to the Land, and to be available as a guide and tutor to those who seek admission to the first level of the Mysteries of the UnderWorld.

Each of these three beings or levels of consciousness are actually part of one another, and all are harmonics of our own inner being. The symbolism and methods implied in *The Prophecies* come from the most potent of these Three Masters: Merlin, the Prophet of the Land. A true inner revolution causes the three levels to merge and become one; in the Grail Mystery all three Achievers would be said to be united in Christ.

The Merlin path, that of the Land, Ancestors, and Under-World, acts as a counterbalance to the escapism and orthodoxy associated with religious mysticism. If we study the medieval legends carefully, we find that the Grail is an UnderWorld vessel of regeneration, and that its great power enabled seekers after enlightenment to become transformed. This counter-balance is not a trivial matter of intellectual abstraction, it is a model for the real presence of our own physical bodies; without the body we have no reality in this world, and no genuine illumination or expanded consciousness will attempt to ignore or reject the human and material world.

In the esoteric traditions, there are realms below or within the Earth, in exactly the same way as there are realms within the human consciousness. Our Figure 9 suggests how these harmonic images relate to one another upon the Tree of Life. This illustration will be very fruitful in any serious meditation upon the enlightenment mediated by Merlin.

To gain the most effective result from imagery of this type, we must grasp it as a holistic pattern. To separate the beings described above and expect them to 'exist' is mere spiritualism, and will only produce trivial imaginative effects. If, however, we truly realize that they are 1: Aspects of ourselves, 2: Aspects of communal consciousness through time, 3: Aspects of archetypical matrices for creation, 4: Historical persons who have become attuned to mythical powers, then we may expect such a holistic approach to generate changes of consciousness within ourselves.

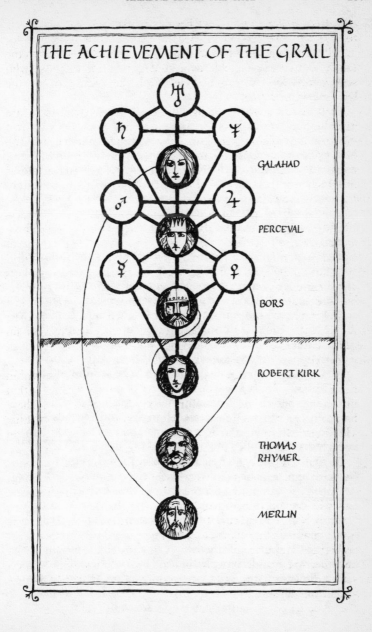

THE ACHIEVEMENT OF THE GRAIL

GALAHAD

PERCEVAL

BORS

ROBERT KIRK

THOMAS
RHYMER

MERLIN

Conclusion: I

The Prophecies of Merlin are a complex collection of mystical, magical, astrological, and predictive sequences, deriving from an ancient oral tradition that permeates western culture, particularly associated with the Britons or Celts. They have been ignored or passed over in modern reassessments of esoteric traditions, and are often regarded as incomprehensible rubbish.

Closer examination of *The Prophecies* reveals the following:

1   A number of magical images, suitable for visualization and meditation. These are allied to traditional and histori-cally proven symbolism reaching back to a pre-Christian era.

2   A clear sequence of prediction from approximately the fifth century to the twenty-first or twenty-second.

3   An apocalyptic vision which holds the key to the primal psychic transformation that was later to be symbolized by the Grail.

4   A number of allegories and images which represent the foundations of traditions attached to the Grail legends.

5   The clearly identifiable fragments of a proto-psychology which may be applied and re-created by anyone seeking to experience the enlightenment of Merlin; which is the enlightenment associated with the ancient traditions of bardship, seership, and prophecy.

6   The remains of a system of astrology that paid particular attention to the seasonal movements of certain observed constellations, and to the Lunar Nodes. As this is not astrology in the modern sense, we might call it symbolic astronomy, as it derives psychic and environmental patterns from direct observation, placing observation before calcula-tion. Calculation, however, must have also played its part.

7   A series of clues that suggest a pattern of cycles and

polarity relationships inherent in the Grail legends, all of which are indicated in *The Prophecies* and the setting for *The Prophecies* within Geoffrey of Monmouth's *History of the Kings of Britain*.

Conclusion: II

REVOLUTIONARY ASPECTS

The Prophecies do not stand in isolation, but derive from both classical and native (Celtic) traditions, curiously intermixed, with a certain amount of Biblical or orthodox religious influence.

In keeping with prophetic material worldwide, we find that Merlin is critical of authority, of the corruption of state religion, and that a revolutionary quality runs through the text. This revolution is primarily an individual or psychic event, but has distinct cultural and political ramifications. In this context, *The Prophecies of Merlin* form part of a long tradition of revolutionary or fundamentally radical reaction, allied to inner vision.

Britain is notorious for material of this sort; a short list would include William Blake, Percy Shelley (though he might have denied such a role), Karl Marx (writing in England): but these titanic figures stand firmly upon a foundation laid by earlier British visionaries. The religious and social revolutionaries such as the Diggers (mid seventeenth century) or Levellers, Abiezer Coppe, and the English Revolution itself, are derived from visionary sources which are too often glossed over by rational economically inclined historians.

This same vision, of unity with a common earth, sometimes of apocalyptic conclusions, inspired early emigrants to the New World. We may find attitudes and symbols that predate such cultural upheavals within *The Prophecies of Merlin*. This is not to suggest that they are *due* to *The Prophecies*, but that the Merlin text expresses certain fundamental insights and responses that are inherent in the British mystical and revolutionary visions throughout the centuries that followed. Prophecy was often a form of propaganda in the ancient and medieval worlds, but there is more than sufficient evidence of the genuine visionary quality of Merlin's verses to enable us to classify them as inner or even spiritual inspirations, rather than mere jargon or wishful thinking. In later centuries 'prophecies' became increasingly propagandist, and were used as psychological weaponry as late as the First and Second World Wars.

We may trace this visionary element to certain concepts which are associated with the Celtic peoples: unity with the Land, property shared in common, or at least in a manner very different from the Roman/capitalist system of ownership, and a firm foundation of poetry and inspired tradition as a basis and guide for everyday life.

In recent years, certain intellectual historians have used this poetic foundation as a basis for political theory (see for example the French writer J.J. Markale) but a reasoned basis, such as that ascribed to political communism, is very different indeed from the intuitive basis which energized early practical Communists.

We would not be too outrageous to remember that Marx drew heavily upon mystical traditions for his work, the result of which has indirectly created vast Communist territories with a political basis that seems little different from a model of orthodoxy based upon religious dogma.

Just as the fundamental mystical communists of seventeenth- and eighteenth-century Britain were ruthlessly destroyed by vested interests, so have the earliest verses that express their vision (those of Merlin) been ignored or forgotten. In the twentieth century we find some of Merlin's most obscure and recondite visions becoming fact; just as the unacceptable social visions of the Diggers are being realized in China or Israel. Today we have lost or outgrown the religious orthodox basis, or have transformed the dogmatic restraints and corruption into politics. Both the social visions of the fundamental communists ('All things in common, all people One . . .'), and the transpersonal visions of Merlin concerning psychic revolution, find expression in contemporary history.

While it is presumptuous to suggest a firm connection between occultism, esoteric lore, and politics, there can be no doubt that certain inner realizations push both individuals and groups to generate dynamic changes in society. In the individual these changes result from a catalytic revolution of consciousness, the peak of which is the prophetic ferment found within the Merlin verses. There are many more acceptable and readily understandable levels of this transaction; in a group it becomes resistance, revolution, protest, experimentation with new social patterns. Sometimes these are successfully imprinted upon the broader society at large. More often they fail through the opposition of fear, greed, and ruthless vested interests.

Curiously, the inertia that dissipates inspired efforts to improve society is that very same inertia which allows development of the weapons of destruction so vividly implied by Merlin's enigmatic verses. Just as the semi-legendary Merlin described by Geoffrey of Monmouth or Nennius was born of a daemon and a virgin, so is the inner Merlin in group or shared consciousness born of abnormal union, generated through stress or conflict.

In this sense, we may employ Merlin, the mysterious prophet who encapsulated the future History of Britain in his verses, as a model or focus for individual and social revolution. In the allegory of Merlin and Vortigern's Tower, the youthful Merlin confronts and confounds the corrupt King and his false advisers; Merlin is truth breaking through the poisonous crust of a polluted society – in this sense he is the youthful revolution that arises with each successive generation, but the communal vision runs deeper and stronger than mere juvenile rebellion that soon, regrettably, subsides.

The mature Merlin, who has undergone the inner ferment set out in the verses of *The Prophecies*, seeks to provide clues for a balanced cultural development, and this is firmly based upon individual psychic transformation. The transformation is well known in oral tradition; it concerns the sanctity of the environment and of life, it involves a realization of the cohering and balancing value of music and poetry as a foundation for human communication, and it demands a continuing insight and searching consciousness, even if such realization leads to the sacrifice of the individual in pursuit of a definition of truth. All of these elements are found in the medieval Merlin verses, rendered into Latin by Geoffrey of Monmouth, but deriving from earlier oral sources.

The obscure poetry of Merlin, much of which is drawn from pre-Christian imagery and the remnants of a pagan culture imprinted upon the medieval communal imagination, advocates a path of constant and ongoing revolution. In *The Prophecies* this revolution is represented by images such as the potent 'goddess of Britain' who purifies lust and death, or the astrological sequence from immutable rigid order to fluid and far-reaching chaos; if we accept that the language and imagery change with the times, the message remains constant: freedom is gained through revolution.

As has been suggested, this revolutionary attitude runs through British social history; if Merlin's predictions are accurate (either in a psychological or historical sense) then we are soon to experience a number of dramatic social upheavals, in which the chaotic but purgative reactions symbolized by the Prophecies will surface into common consciousness and action.

There is a general (inaccurate) tendency to link ancient texts, so-called esoteric lore, and predictive verses, with extreme right-wing reactionary or even fascist politics. Innumerable fanciful tales are related concerning Hitler's obsession with occult matters, and there can be little doubt that there is some truth in this theme, but only from the viewpoint of groups and individuals who lust after power − exactly in the manner represented by the usurping King Vortigern in Geoffrey's allegory of overbalanced greed, lust and pretension.

The truth of the matter seems to be the opposite to that customary and rather facile belief: genuine 'esoteric' or prophetic and visionary consciousness is the origin of the fundamental left-wing in modern politics, and may be traced socially through each century, until it reaches the medieval *Prophecies*, or even earlier prophetic texts which were influential upon medieval writers.

CREATION OF THE WORLDS

APPENDIX I
The Creation of the World

Merlin's final vision is clarified by the creation sequence found in the *Vita Merlini*, Geoffrey's most enigmatic work relating to our British prophet.

Although the sources for this fourfold elemental symbolism were part of the scholar's education of the twelfth century, they in turn devolve from magical or metaphysical models of very ancient origins.

Despite evidence that Geoffrey is likely to have drawn upon the work of Isidore of Seville, and upon Bede's *De Natura Rerum*, there is a strong likelihood that this Creation of the World also includes an oral teaching, a wisdom poem from Welsh or Breton tradition.

The structure is similar to those that later developed in the Cabalistic traditions in Europe, wherein the Four Elements (shown here by the four original prior causes) combine to generate more complex shapes. If we follow the imagery closely, it is found to hold the typical mirroring of greater and lesser Worlds, the Macrocosmos and the Microcosmos. Figure 10 shows that the Earth with its four winds, seas, and five-fold global division reflects the greater pattern of the four-fold Creation, in which the world sits as a fifth unity in the centre.

This traditional pattern of Creation is also the pattern for the individual psyche in the old magical systems. It has further links with the subtle currents of the psychic-body complex, shown in esoteric teachings by the various inner power-centres, or by the meridians taught in traditional acupuncture in the east.

The Goddess Ariadne lives in the very heart of this web of interactions, and when Merlin tells us that 'the clash of the Winds shall be heard among the Stars',[1] we should refer to this cosmological model.

Extract from the *Vita Merlini* of Geoffrey of Monmouth,

translated by J.J. Parry, University of Illinois, 1925:

Meanwhile Taliesin had come to see Merlin the prophet who had sent for him to find out what wind or rainstorm was coming up, for both together were drawing near and the clouds were thickening. He drew the following illustrations under the guidance of Minerva his associate.

'Out of nothing the Creator of the world produced four [elements] that they might be the prior cause as well as the material for creating all things when they were joined together in harmony: the heaven which He adorned with stars and which stands on high and embraces everything like the shell surrounding a nut; then He made the air, fit for forming sounds, through the medium of which day and night present the stars; the sea which girds the land in four circles, and with its mighty refluence so strikes the air as to generate the winds which are said to be four in number; as a foundation He placed the earth, standing by its own strength and not lightly moved, which is divided into five parts, whereof the middle one is not habitable because of the heat and the two furthest are shunned because of their cold. To the last two He gave a moderate temperature and these are inhabited by men and birds and herds of wild beasts. He added clouds to the sky so that they might furnish sudden showers to make the fruits of the trees and of the ground grow with their gentle sprinkling. With the help of the sun these are filled like water skins from the rivers by a hidden law, and then, rising through the upper air, they pour out the water they have taken up, driven by the force of the winds. From them come rainstorms, snow, and round hail when the cold damp wind breathes out its blasts which, penetrating the clouds, drive out the streams just as they make them. Each of the winds takes to itself a nature of its own from its proximity to the zone where it is born. Beyond the firmament in which He fixed the shining stars He placed the ethereal heaven and gave it as a habitation to troops of angels whom the worthy contemplation and marvellous sweetness of God refresh throughout the ages. This also He adorned with stars and the shining sun, laying down the law, by which the star should run within fixed limits through the part of heaven entrusted to it. He afterwards placed beneath this the airy heavens, shining with the lunar body, which throughout their high places abound in troops of spirits who sympathize or rejoice with us as things go well or ill. They are accustomed to carry the prayers of men through the air and to beseech God to have mercy on them, and to bring back intimations of God's will, either in dreams or by voice or by other signs, through doing which they become wise. The space beyond the moon abounds in evil demons, who are skilled to cheat and deceive and tempt us; often they assume a body made of air and appear to us and many things often follow. They even hold intercourse with women and make them pregnant, generating in an unholy manner. So therefore He made the heavens to be inhabited by three orders of spirits that each one might look out for something and renew the world from the renewed seed of things.'[2]

APPENDIX II
'Woe's me for the Red Dragon'

Thomas Heywood's *Interpretation of Merlin's Prophecies*, as a 'Chronographical History of all the Kings and memorable Passages of this Kingdom, from Brute to the reign of King Charles the First' (First published in 1641, republished in 1812, at Carmarthen).

Thomas Heywood's book is remarkable in several respects, for it contains an English verse translation of *The Prophecies* (most of which bears no relationship to the Latin text of Geoffrey, due to imaginative expansion) and a summary of the various Histories and Chronicles, correlated up to the reign of Charles I with Merlin's verses.

The 1812 edition contains a number of translations of Welsh poems relating to Merlin and Taliesin, which have been added by the publisher, based upon a translation of the *Myvyrian Archaeology of Wales*, from *Pugh's British and Out-landish Prophecies*. None of these relates to the *Prophecies of Merlin*, however, though they do have some relationship to the *Vita Merlini*. Heywood amplified his 'Chronographical History' with numerous anecdotes, items of folklore, and a strongly imaginative style of writing. The two extracts appended here include verses which are clearly translations of the medieval Merlin text of Geoffrey, and Heywood's re-telling of the story of Fair Rosamund. This second item has curious mythological overtones, and Rosamund 'The Rose of the World' is the English version of Ariadne, the classical goddess of the Thread, who appears in the closing vision of *The Prophecies*.

Cross references to the verse numbers used in my own commentary appear (where possible) to the right of Heywood's poetry.

Woe's me for the red Dragon, for alach,
The time is come, hee hasteth to his mach:
The bloody Serpent, (yet whose souls are white)
Implys that Nation, on which they delight
Was late sole-fixt, (the *Saxon*) who as friends
Came to thee first, but ayming at shrewd ends
They shall have power over the drooping *red*,
In which the British Nation's figured:
Drive shall he them into caves, holes, and
   dens,
To barren Mountain, and to moorish fens,   *Verses 1-3*
Hills shall remove to where the valleyes
   stood,
And all the baths and brooks shall flow with
   blood.
The worship of the holy God shall cease.
For in thilk dayes the Kirke shall have no
   peace:
The Panims (woe the while) shall get the day,
And with their Idols mawmetry beare
   sway,
And yet in fine shee that was so opprest,
Shal mount, & in the high rocks build her
   nest.
For out of *Cornwall* shall proceed a Bore,
Who shall the Kerk to pristine state restore,
Bow shall all *Britaine* to his kingly beck,
And tread he shall on the white Dragon's
   neck.

But well-away for thee, to *Britaine* deere,
For I fore-see thy sad disaster's neere.

Fly from these fatall severall fires o King,
Which from less *Britain* the two exiles bring:
Now are their ships a rigging, now forsake,
Th' *Armoricke* shoares, and towards *Albion* make,
To avenge their murdered brothers bloud on
   thee,
In *Totnesse* road to morrow they will bee,

4 who

4 y

The *Saxon* Princes shall contend in vain,
For young *Aurelius* having *Hengist* slain,
Shall peaceably possesse the *British* throne,
Striving the opposite Nations to attone.
He the true faith shall seek to advance on
     high,
But in the quest thereof, by poyson die,
The Dragons head, his brother shall succeed,
And after many a brave heroick deed,
By him perform'd, the fates shall strive to
     waft,
His soule ore Styx, by a like poysnous
     draught,
But those who sent them to th' *Elizian*
     bower,
His sonne the Bore of *Cornwall* shall devoure.

The *Cornish Bore* shall fill with his
     devotion,
The Christian World: the Islands of the
     Ocean,
He shall subdue: the Flower de Lyces plant,
In his own Garden, and prove Paramant,
The two-neckt *Roman* Eagle hee shall make
To flag her plumes, and her faint feathers
     quake.
Pagans shall strive in vain to bend or break
     him,
Who shall be meat to all the mouths that
     speake him,
Yet shall his end be doubtfull: Him six Kings
Shall orderly succeed, but when their wings
Are clipt by death, a *German* Worme shall
     rise
Who shall the *British* State anatomise.
Him, shall a Sea-Wolfe waited on by Woods
From *Africke* brought to pass Saint *Georges*
     floods
Advance on high: then shall Religion faile,
And then shall *London's* Clergie honour
     vaile

Versification of
'HISTORIA'

Verses 3-6

To *Dorobernia*: he that seventy shall sit
In th' *Eboraúcensick* Sea, he forc'd to flit
Into *Armorica: Menevia* sad
Shall with the Legion Cities Pall be clad,
And they that in thilk days shall live, may see
That all these changes in the Kirke shall bee.

The Heavens in stead of water, bloud shall
   showre,
And famine shall both young and old
   devoure:
Droop and be sad shall the *red Dragon then*,
But after mickle time be blithe agen,
And now the Serpent that was white before,
Shall have his silver scales, and drencht in
   gore.
Seven scepter-bearing Kings in field shall die,   *Verses 6-8*
One of whose Sainted soules shall pierce the
   skie,
Kept shall the babes bee from their Mothers
   wombes:
And soone as climbe, on earth, grope from
   their Tombes.
All by a brazen man shall come to passe,
Who likewise mounted on his Steed of
   brasse,
Both night and day will *Londons* prime
   Gate keep,
Whether the carlesse people wake or sleep.

The crimson Dragon with his own fierce
   pawes
Shall teare his proper bowels 'gainst
   the Laws:
Of wholesome Nature, plague, and famine
   then
Shall fill the barren earth with shrowds
   of men.
After, the Dragon whose smooth scales are
   white,
Hither the *Almans* daughter shall invite,

And crown themselves: Against whom shall
    rise
An Eagle from the Rock, and both surprise,
Two Lions shall a dreadful combat make,
Having their Lists encompast by a Lake.   ·
At length be atton'd, and after shall divide,   *Verses 8-13*
The glorious prey: aspeckled scale, whose
    pryde,
Shall ayme at high things; will his Lord
    betray
Poysoning the Royal nest in which he lay
Of the white Dragon, so the Fates agree,
At length a *Decemvirum* there shall be:
What time the Red shall to his joy behold
The roofs of all his Temples deckt with
    gold, &c.

And *Helluo* then with open jaws shall
    yawne,
And he an *Hydra* with seven heads shall
    grace,
Glad to behold the ruine of his race,
And then upon the *Neustrian* bloud shall
    prey,
And tithe them by the pole (now well away)
Burst shall he after gorg'd with humane
    blood,
And leave his name in part of the salt flood.
Iron men, in woodden Tents shall here arrive,
And hence the *Saxons* with her Eglets
    drive, &c.   *Verses 13-17*

He that Iron Nation who leads forth for
    prey,
Shall find full spoils, and where he feeds will
    stay:
Suppressing the red *Dragon* for a space.
Then shall arise two *Dragons* from his race:
One, aymes at, but attains not his desire.
By Envies Dart the other shall expire.
The *Lion* next of *Justice* must appeare,

Who 'gainst the *Celticke* Towers will ladders
  reare.
And cause the Lily like the Aspen shake,
Whose rore shall all the Island Serpents quake.
(A cunning Alcumist) who hath the skill,
Gold, both from flowers, and Nettles to distill.

'To prophets there be several attributes given, some are called prophatae, some vates, others videntes; this is prophets, predictors, and seers. The name of prophets was, and ought to be peculiar to those that dealt only in divine mysteries, and spake to the people the words which the Almighty did dictate unto them concerning those things which should futurely happen . . .' Heywood, Chapter One. (1812)

Heywood makes a threefold division, the same division represented by the Three Orders or Worlds of 'Spiritual Beings' in the Creation sequence from the *Vita Merlini*.

This threefold distinction is of a traditional origin, but is continually encountered within explorations of the human psyche. In orthodox religion, we have the Holy Trinity; in the Grail legends the Three Achievers; in pagan mysteries the Three Mothers; in the traditions of the UnderWorld three levels or modes of consciousness are repeatedly reported.

FAIR ROSAMUND

Henry, in the fourteenth year of his reign, caused his eldest son Henry, to be crowned king of England, at Westminster, giving him full power over the realm, whilst he himself was negotiated in Normandy, and his many other provinces, which after proved to his great disadvantage and trouble. In which interim, he had cast his eye upon a most beautiful lady, called Rosamond, on whom he was so greatly enamoured, that it grew even to a dotage, so that he neglected the queen's company, insomuch, that she incensed all his sons, who took up arms against their father in the quarrel of their mother, by which, the peace of the land was turned to hostility and uproar; yet, the king so far prevailed, that he surprised the queen, and kept her in close prison, and withal, was so indulgent over his new mistress, that he built for her a rare and wonderous fabrick, so curiously devised, and intricated with so many turning meanders and winding indents, that none, upon any occasion, might have access unto her, unless directed by the king, or such as in that business he most trusted. And this edifice he erected at Woodstock, not far from Oxford, and made a labyrinth which was wrought like a knot in a garden, called a maze, in which any one might loose himself, unless guided by a line or thread, which, as it guided him in, so it directed him the way out. But, in process, it so happened, that the sons having the better of their father, set at liberty their mother, who, when the king was absent came secretly to Woodstock with her train, at such a time, when the knight, her guardian being out of the way, not dreaming of any such accident, had left the clue carelessly and visible in the entrance of the labyrinth.

Which the queen espying, slipped not that advantage, but wound herself by that silken thread even to the very place where she found her sitting, and presenting her with a bowl of poison, she compelled her to drink it off in her presence, after which draught, she within few minutes expired, and the queen departed from thence in her revenge fully satisfied, for which cruel act, the king could never be drawn to reconcile himself unto her afterwards, and this makes good that of Merlin:

> ———of all the flowers that grow,
> The Rose shall most delight his scent: and so
> That lest it any strangers eyes should daze,
> He plants it close in a *Dedalian* Maze.

Rosamond being dead, was buried in the monastery of Godstow, near unto Oxford, upon whose tomb was inscribed:

> *Ilic jacent in tumba, Rosamundi non Rosamund:*
> *Non redolent, sed olet, quœ redolere solet.*

Which, by an ancient writer was thus paraphrased into English:

> *The Rose of the World, but not the clean flower*

Is graven here, to whom beauty was lent
In this grave full darke, now is her bower
That in her life was sweet and redolent:
But now that she is from this life blent,
Though she were sweet, now fouly doth she stink,
A mirrour good for all that on her think.

Such was their English poetry in those days. Long after the death of Rosamond, was shewed in that abbey a rare coffer or casket of hers, about two feet in length, in which was a strange artificial motion, where were to be seen giants fighting, beasts in motion, fowls flying, and fishes swimming.

APPENDIX III
Places names in The Prophecies

The use of place names in the text of *The Prophecies* has been touched upon in several examples in the preceding chapters. These examples reveal a pattern in the use of such names, which may be briefly summarized as follows:

1 *Names from traditional and chronicle sources*

A number of the places named are obviously drawn from sources such as Nennius or Bede, and the appearance of Snowdon (Mons Eris and other variants) is a good example of this, appearing as it does in the allegory of Vortigern's Tower (amplified by Geoffrey from the version told by Nennius) and in the verses of *The Prophecies* themselves.

2 *Names of locations of national or contemporary importance*

These include London, Winchester, Gloucester, and other towns or regions which are instantly recognizable. It seems more than likely that Geoffrey has introduced many of these to give an air of contemporary meaning for his listeners; we have no way of knowing if such names were, in fact, original to the oral sources on which Geoffrey's text is based, and this application of names leads us to (3).

3 *Names used in a symbolic manner*

This category overlaps with (2) above, for politically significant cities such as Winchester are clearly used to symbolize the qualities that they represented in the contemporary imagination. The allegory of the Three Fountains, for example (verse 42), employs Winchester as its location, yet it is clearly a motif drawn from Celtic tradition.

4 *Obscure place names*

A number of names are derived from small locations in

Monmouthshire or other parts of Wales. The River Periron (verse 27) is a tributary of the Monmow, and would not have been known to many of Geoffrey's readers or listeners. The fountain of Galabes, the River Amne, and various other names seem to be deliberately localized and obscure.

There are two possible sources for such names. The first is oral tradition, in which Geoffrey follows the principle of not changing names which are already contained within a known source; in his case the verses in the British tongue which he drew upon for his Latin version of *The Prophecies*. There is some evidence that Geoffrey employed traditional place names even when he was unsure of their actual location or meaning.

Second, Geoffrey may have been following an ancient tradition of localizing place names within a magical landscape. This is particularly noticeable in verses where powerful magical or prophetic images are related to obscure place names. The choice of certain names of small rivers or localities from Monmouthshire suggests that Geoffrey, or a local oral source such as a bard, has used a familiar landscape in the manner of a symbolic topography.

This is not an unusual practice, and a number of similar patterns are found in other regions of Britain, upheld by local tradition even today. A mythical or even a distant historical event or series of events is located to a particular region in the popular imagination. In Glastonbury, in Somerset, for example, the Grail legends are related to the landscape, and a modern variant of the same traditional practice now seeks to add Zodiacal attributes to the list. Ancient earthworks and sites in the region have consistently fired the imagination, and such images are upheld by continuing traditions. In the Lowlands of Scotland, we find the mystical geography of Thomas Rhymer, the site of his magical Hawthorn Tree (blown down in the nineteenth century), the Eildon Hills where he disappeared into Faeryland, and the numerous localities mentioned in Thomas's *Prophecies*, including a site called 'Merlin's Grave'. In Bath, site of the famous Baths and Temple of Aquae Sulis, we find the legend of King Bladud, a Druidical King, necromancer and aviator, written upon the local landscape, and tied to local legends of his magical cure in the healing springs.

The Prophecies of Merlin, however, cover the entire country of Britain; it is likely that when in doubt over the locality of a vision, Geoffrey or his source placed it upon the local landscape for reference. In some magical systems, the land is used as a mnemonic for a psychic topology. In this context, we must realize that localized myths always have a transcendent level of meaning, either transpersonal or Seasonal or Stellar; we may choose which level we respond to or recognize.

A detailed study of the place names in Geoffrey's *History* is found in Tatlock 1950.

Notes

INTRODUCTION

1 Apuleius, *De Deo Socratis*, Ch.6. In medieval works the classical variants of the motif are frequently combined with native beliefs which derive from Otherworld and Ancestor cults and practices. Both native and classical Greek or Roman examples of this belief have a common symbolic and primitive cultural background.

2 Michel de Notredame, 1503-66. Astrologer, physician, seer. Although a great deal of nonsense has been written about Nostradamus, his own 'Preface à mon fils' dated 1 March 1555 reveals a deep insight into the nature of prophecy.

3 Helena Petrovna Blavatsky. Nineteenth century. Popularly known as the founder of the Theosophical Society. Despite the strongly intellectual re-workings of eastern mysticism and religion for which she is famous, Blavatsky was also an active practitioner of western ritual magic. As such she exercised a profound influence over the development of nineteenth-century esoteric orders, many of which derived membership or leadership from her own 'secret lodge'.

4 Rudolf Steiner. Nineteenth to twentieth century. Founder of the Anthroposophical Society, separated from the Theosophists. Steiner is the intellectual and esoteric genius of our era, and embodies the power of seership allied to practical work.

5 Thomas Rhymer, Thomas of Erceldoune, Lord Learment, or 'True' Thomas. A nineteenth-century Scot, author of an early version of 'Tristram' and of various prophetic verses. Associated with Thomas is the oral ballad 'Thomas the Rhymer' and a Romance. Both tell of a magical initiation in the world of Faery, or the UnderWorld, whereby the individual is given prophetic sight. Thomas's prophecies were published regularly until as late as the nineteenth century, and were known to Shakespeare who incorporated certain verses into his plays.

The initiation of Thomas in Faeryland is one of the major esoteric key visions deriving from ancient oral tradition. Like both Merlin and King Arthur, Thomas is said to live on in the hollow Eildon hills of his homeland in southern Scotland, a nationalist hero, seer, and potential saviour.

6 Reverend Robert Kirk. Born 1644. Author of *The Secret Commonwealth*: a study of the realm of supernatural beings in Gaelic speaking Scotland. Kirk translated the Psalms, Catechism, and Bible into Gaelic. Rumoured even to this day to be alive in Faeryland, attempts to 'rescue' Kirk have been made by people in his native Aberfoyle within living memory. (Ed. Sanderson, Folklore Society.)

7 Geoffrey drew upon the sources of Gildas, Nennius, Bede, and other chronicles. He also states that British history was circulated 'Iocunde' or jocularly by word of mouth among the people.

8 Translations: Giles, 1848/1896; Evans, 1912; Griscom, 1929; Thorpe, 1966. Also Heywood, 1641 (1812); Thompson, 1718. Heywood contains an expanded metrical translation.

9 This relationship becomes clear in the larger context of *The History*. *The History* and *The Prophecies* should both be read for full appreciation of the interconnections.

10 Giles, op. cit.

11 Rees 1978; Ross 1974; MacCana 1975.

12 Knight 1983.

13 Matarasso (trans.) 1969.

1 MERLIN, MAKER AND TUTOR OF KINGS

1 Matthews (ed.) 1984.

2 The Three Achievers of the Grail are aspects of the nature of Christ, and so are acceptable to orthodox religion. They are reflected or balanced, however, by three figures who dwell in the Celtic UnderWorld. (See Chapter 10.)

2 THE BREATH OF PROPHECY

1 A literary study of *The Prophecies* is made by Tatlock, 1950. See page 405, Ch. XVII.

2 Geoffrey states that his edition of *The Prophecies* is made by public demand, and at the request of his patron.

3 Davidson 1971.

4 Tatlock cites the classical sources.

5 Ross 1974: 265-301. Henderson in Jung/Franz 1979 gives a short psychological summary of mythical themes.

6 Wentz; W. Y. Evans 1909; Johnson 1775; Campbell 1900, 1902; Kirk 1692.

7 Tart 1975, Chapters 1-2; Govinda 1969, p. 159; Nostradamus, *Preface à mon fils*: 'Although, indeed, now or hereafter some persons may arrive to whom God Almighty may be pleased to reveal by imaginative impression some secrets of the future, as accorded in time past to judicial astrology, that a certain power and volitional faculty came upon them, as a flame of fire appears.' (1555)

8 Knight 1983:177-219. Govinda 1969:190-8.

9 Jung 1979: 196-8.

10 See Appendix II and Chapter 10.

3   THE INNER STRUCTURE OF *THE PROPHECIES*: I

1 Tatlock 1950.

2 Thorpe 1978: 47,246-51.

3 Gantz 1976: 9-34.

4 Thorpe 1978: 117-18.

5 'Walter, Archdeacon of Oxford, a man of great eloquence and learning in foreign histories, offered me a very ancient book in the British tongue which in a continued and regular story and elegant style related the actions of them all (i.e. the Kings) from Brutus, the first King of the Britons, down to Cadwallader the son of Cadwallo . . .' *British History*, translated Aaron Thompson, 1718.

6 The tone of *The Prophecies* is condemnatory. Church practices and corruption are attacked, while Christian dogma or salvation are ignored.

7 Coleman 1964.

8 Mann 1979; Knight 1978.

9 Stewart 1985.

4   THE INNER STRUCTURE OF *THE PROPHECIES*: II

1 Early commentaries were particularly prone to an apparently credulous reading of *The Prophecies*. We must consider these, however, in the ambience of the religion and culture of the period, and not read them as literal examples of medieval willingness to believe in total correlation or pin-point prediction. The symbolic *pattern* of order was more important in this context than the factual correspondence, and if a prediction did not seem to fit with an ordered world-view, then it was altered or interpreted to make

it fit. This medieval obsession with pattern and order is particularly significant when we consider that sections of *The Prophecies* are far removed from accepted medieval secular or religious imagery.

2 This orthodox suppression followed from the earlier imperial destruction of the Druids by Rome, and in a poetic and cultural sense is a direct harmonic of the Roman conquest and proscription of Druidism.

3 Tatlock 1950 cites comparable prophetic texts.

4 The aim of Geoffrey's *History* was to establish the lineage of the British people, from the mythical Brutus to the last British king, Cadwallader, in the seventh century.

5 See Tatlock for an analysis of many of Geoffrey's paraphrases.

6 Tatlock, op. cit.

7 Thorpe 1978:246-51.

8 Isaiah XIII,10; Joel II,10; Mark XIII, 24-5; Rev.VI, 13, XII, 4.

9 Geoffrey quotes from the *Pharsalia* (IV, 7 and 9) and mentions Lucan by name. See Graves 1956.

10 The *Oracula Sibyllina* were written some time during the first century. Geoffrey has one of his characters (XII,18) take a number of prophetic books and read them: *The Auguries of the Shaftesbury Eagle; The Sayings of The Sibyl;* and of course *The Prophecies of Merlin.*

11 Tatlock, op. cit.

12 Child, number 37.

13 Apuleius, *The Golden Ass.*

14 Brennan 1983; Graves 1961; Stewart 1981.

15 Examples are found in Godwin 1979; short studies of the cosmologies of Robert Fludd and Atharasius Kircher. Most modern metaphysical diagrams and models are restatements of Renaissance originals.

16 There is some implication of triadic form in the verses rendered into Latin by Geoffrey; the triad was the traditional structure for Druidic lore.

17 MacCana 1975; Sharkey 1975; Rees 1961.

18 In the later sections of *The Prophecies*, we find naked men riding upon serpents, an unusual image for medieval poetry. One of the heroes in *The Prophecies* is stronger when naked than when clothed, a characteristic of the berserker, and of the ancient Celts who are described by classical writers as charging naked into battle. The images may therefore be a re-working of hero-tales from oral tradition, and this same element of imagery is likely to have stimulated many of the bizarre tales related to witchcraft.

19 Matarasso 1969: 9-29.

20 Irish parallels are found in the ancient poems: 'The Dialogue of the Two Sages'; 'Prophecy of Conn'; 'Prophecy of The Champion'; 'Prophecy of Art'. (Eugene O'Curry, 'Lectures on the Manuscript Materials of Ancient Irish History', Dublin, 1873.) In Wales, the 'Black Book of Carmarthen'; 'The Book of Taliesin' and a prophecy in the 'History of Gruffydd ap Cynan' are typical examples. Scotland's 'Thomas Rhymer' has been referred to above, and the native Scottish Merlin traditions are found in Parry 1925.

21 Tatlock, op. cit.

22 Rees 1961.

23 Spence.

24 Book of Revelation.

25 Tatlock, op. cit.

5   MERLIN AND VORTIGERN

1 This nonsensical theory began with the nineteenth-century Theosophical Society, and was maintained well into the middle of the twentieth century.

2 Tradition asserts that there is a bottomless bog on Snowdon, which swallowed up a town. On Dinas Emrys (one of the sites traditionally associated with Merlin) there are the remains of a building, and a marshy area deriving from several seeping springs. In Brittany the famous legend of Ys, which sank beneath the sea for its wickedness, is a Celtic parallel of the Biblical Tower of Babel motif.

3 Dragons have a particular connection with the geomantic power of the earth; in both eastern and western cultures, the dragon is a symbol of energies that flow across and within the landscape. Parallels are found in the 'Serpent Power' of Kundalini yoga, in which vital energies are aroused within the physical body, but attuned to a psychic or spiritual aim.

4 The Empire proscribed human sacrifice in the first century B.C. The Celts were notorious to the classical writers for the practice of preserving heads in cedar oil and carrying out human sacrifices.

5 Ross 1974.

6 Both Merlin and Arthur are born in rather similar circumstances. Both mothers conceive as the result of a mysterious male visitor. In a mythical sense, Arthur is a harmonic or similar being to Merlin. Arthur's power is expressed through kingship, whereas Merlin's is through prophecy.

7 Parry 1925.

8 In Gerald's *Conquest of Ireland* he states that four Irish prophets

foretell the English conquest, but not until the day of judgment. They are Columkill, Berchan, Patrick, and Moling; all are Catholic saints, however. He also tells us that prophecies were 'still carried in the memory of bards' and quotes material which is both from *The Prophecies of Merlin* and from other obscure sources. In addition to quoting Merlin, Merlin Silverstris, and defending god-given powers of prophecy Gerald also mentions Meilerius, a seer of his own day.

9 *History* (IX,17;XII,18).

10 A strong pattern of unorthodox symbolism is found in medieval material, in which magical, meditative, and other techniques of transforming consciousness are revealed. Many of the famous texts such as the Mabinogion, the Grail legends, collected Welsh and Irish tales, even the *History of the British Kings*, all contain material which derives from pre-Christian cultural sources.

11 Tatlock, p. 63.

12 These twelve images are similar in many ways to the visual keys found in Tarot and other traditional pictures employed to alter modes of consciousness.

13 Read 1961.

14 Mark 13, 22-7; II Peter 2, 1; Exodus 9; Genesis 41,8 and 24; Daniel 2,27.

15 Ferrex and Porrex, II,16. Belinus and Brennus, III,1. Arthgallo and Elidurus, III,16-17. Cadwallo and Edwinus, XII,3.

16 Nennius states outright that the mother of Merlin was a virgin.

17 It is Vortigern who asks what would later be known as 'the Grail Question': 'What does it mean? . . .' thus stimulating the youthful Merlin's prophetic trance. *The Prophecies* as a whole may be regarded as a primal and extended version of the wonders of the Vision of the Grail.

18 In Irish hero tales, the concept of *geis* or *gessa* is a direct parallel from an early culture. (See Rees 1961, 231, 260, 282, 294, 327, 348.) In oral tradition, murder for ritual or magical reasons seems to be attended by a *geis* of confession or revelation.

19 A number of poems in Welsh are extant, attributed to this bard, but may well be derived from undatable oral traditions, similar to those employed by Geoffrey of Monmouth. (Lady Charlotte Guest 1904)

20 Images of this sort were to flourish in alchemical texts not long after Geoffrey was writing, and had a lengthy currency up to the eighteenth or even nineteenth century.

21 A Freudian psychologist might find an inevitable phallic and sexual symbolism in this sequence of images; but in the ancient metaphysics the genital organs were merely one natural expression

of archetypical patterns of polarity.

22 There are a number of localities in which Gates to the UnderWorld traditionally exist. The siting of the Temple of Sulis Minerva at Bath, England, is one of the best researched pagan sites, but many folk tales are found in Scotland, Wales, Ireland, and Brittany that repeat the theme of an UnderWorld gate. During a visit to Brittany in 1979, I stayed near a place called 'The Gate of Hell', which is a marshy region close to the inland Mont St Michel. Like the British site of Glastonbury Tor, this location had once been associated with the Wild Hunt, in which spirits are carried off through a magical gateway to the Otherworld or UnderWorld.

23 Govinda 1969. Numerous popular works on Kundalini yoga exist.

24 The significance of a particular question is found throughout magical and metaphysical symbolism and in many initiatory texts.

25 Tatlock, p. 364.

26 'SPIRIT. In Hebrew, Ruach: in Greek, Pneuma. In scripture the word Spirit is taken 1) For the Holy Ghost . . . who inspired the Prophets, animates good men . . . the Holy Ghost is called Spirit, being as it were breathed, and proceeding from the Father and Son who inspire and move our hearts by him . . .' Cruden 1817.

7 THE INTERPRETATION OF THE PROPHECIES, SIXTH TO TWENTY-FIRST CENTURIES AD

1 In some cases the poetry is so stylized in the translations, that a restatement of the basic imagery has been made. This is not in the form of an academic re-translation, but a restoration in the light of the symbols, modifications typical to Geoffrey (such as his deliberate use of localized place names), and comparable material from other medieval and traditional sources. Where re-statements have been made, the Giles translations always precede them.

2 Merlin is later associated with the removal of the Giant's Dance or Stonehenge from Ireland to England. This curious tradition, reworked by Geoffrey, offers a significant relationship between the prophet Merlin and the ancient stone and earthworks of our prehistoric culture.

3 Nennius. Heywood (1812) for elaborations on this theme.

4 Arthur's kingship is clearly intended to be everything that Vortigern's was not; yet both fail through misunderstanding of the magical polarities aligned to sexuality. Vortigern's failure is through lust, while Arthur's is through innocence and misplaced purity.

5 See above, Ch.3, Note 5.

6 Geoffrey, however, is politially pro-Norman in his overall attitude. The ambiguity of Geoffrey's nationalism has not been sufficiently studied to draw firm conclusions about his personal beliefs.

7 Maglocunus is called Maelgwn by Nennius. He was a king of the North Britons, linked to the Scottish legend of Kentigern, a Merlin story from the thirteenth century. This northern variant of the Merlin legend gives some valuable insights into the relationship between pagan and Christian attitudes. See Ratcliffe Barnett 1937, Ch. 7; Parry 1925.

8 *History*, IX, Ch. 12.

9 Thorpe 1978: 9-22.

10 This theme is found in the Life of Gildas, and in the Life of St David which would have been familiar to the reader or listener attending to *The Prophecies* (Cymmrodor, XXIV,8).

11 Irish retains this quality of inflection even today; many Oriental languages are intimately related to pitch.

12 Geoffrey is apparently influenced in his imagery by accounts of ancient tombs in Rome (Tatlock 1950).

13 Gantz 1976.

14 Tatlock, op. cit.

15 Tatlock, p. 75.

16 Fons Amne (the fountain of the River Amne) is a small location in Monmouthshire.

17 The North is the magical realm of Justice in the British tradition. North features as the area from which retribution comes in *The Prophecies*; in general magical symbolism, North is the Quarter associated with Law, the Element of Earth, powers of purification, reflection, and death.

18 A number of visions take the form of Trees in medieval and early symbolism; this motif derives from the generation symbol known as the Tree of Life. In British legends the Tree is seen as a living tree, while in later images derived from near-Eastern sources it gradually becomes a mathematical symbol, the Qabalistic model employed by Renaissance philosophers.

8   THE SECOND SEQUENCE: IMAGES BEYOND TIME

1 Ross 1974; Rees 1961.

2 Evans Wentz 1957.

3 The Christians believed in a bodily resurrection for the elect. To the pagans the earth was a gateway to the Otherworld.

4 Davis, E. 1804. Graves drew much of *The White Goddess* from this source.

5 Stewart 1981.
6 Read 1961.
7 Tatlock 1950.
8 In the Scottish ballad the 'Lailly Worm' a Serpent coils around a Tree, and slays seven knights. Child, number 36.
9 Thorpe 1978.

9   THE APOCALYPTIC VISION: STELLAR AND PSYCHIC TRANSFORMATION

1 Steiner 1907.
2 Tatlock 1950.
3 'Splendor solis electro Mecurii languebit' refers to the fact that amber is governed by Mercury a Greek astrological attribute – Stilbon, a Greek name meaning glittering, said by Firmicus Maternus to be used by the Egyptians . . . this is more often used as an astronomical or astrological term, rather than poetic or mythological. (Tatlock.)
4 Tatlock, op. cit.
5 Mann 1979; Lilly (ed.) 'Zadkiel' 1913.
6 Bailey, A.
7 West and Toonder 1970.
8 Diodorus Siculus quotes from the lost 'Circuit of the Earth' by Hecataeus (c.500 BC) in which the Greeks link Apollo with the Hyperborean lands of his mother Leto. Here was a circular stone temple, to which the god returned every nineteen years to the music of the harp.
9 Ross 1974: 224, 257, 213-14, 314.
10 Characters relating to Wayland include Tubal-Cain, Daedulus, Quezalcoatl: all uphold traditions of gigantic power, related to metallurgy. The giant being has two aspects, one of destructive power, the other of creative power.
11 The Egyptian Book of the Dead.
12 Kircher, 'Turris Babel'; see Godwin 1979.
13 Derived from the Akkadian name URUANNA, the Light of Heaven, the Sun.
14 The value of the Pleiades to early cultures is an international example of stellar symbolism being employed for magical purposes.
15 Richard Hinckley Allen (1963); Peter Lum (London).
16 The major centre for worship of Neith or Neitha was Säis in lower Egypt. During her annual festival, countless lamps were lit in her honour. Both Proclus and Plutarch tell us that her temple was

inscribed: 'I am all that has been, that is, and that will be; no man
has lifted my Veil. The Sun was my child'
17 Lum, op. cit.

10   ARIADNE CLOSES THE GATE

1 As with all classical deities quoted in a native (British) context, we
must remember that the name describes the *function* and not a
literal reference to the actual Roman or Greek deity described. The
function and attributes of Janus are as follows: Presiding over the
beginning and ending of all events, from which comes the name for
January, the first month of the year. In Rome the first hour of the
day was dedicated to Janus, he was the first addressed in all
solemn sacrifices, and had the title of Father. Traditionally the
Romans said that Janus was in Italy before any of the other gods;
his festival was New Year's Day. Images of Janus show him
bearing a sceptre in the right hand and a key in the left, while
sitting upon a glittering throne. He has two faces, youthful and
aged, looking forward and behind. Other images show Janus with
Four Faces, one to each Quarter of the World. He presided over
the Golden Age of the Latins, sometimes represented as co-ruler
with Saturn. All passages are under the guardianship of Janus; a
door was called a *janua* and an open arched passage a *janus*.
2 Graves 1961, p. 178.
3 Stewart 1985.
4 Apuleius, *The Golden Ass*.
5 Ariadne was the daughter of King Minos, who sacrificed youths
and maidens to a monster called the Minotaur, half man and half
bull. Ariadne provided Theseus with a length of thread by which
he found his way out of the Labyrinth after slaying the Minotaur.
Theseus took Ariadne with him, but abandoned her on the island
of Naxos. There she was found by Bacchus, who married her and
presented her with a golden crown made by Hephaestus. This
crown was later transformed into a constellation.
6 Ariadne is related to Minerva or Athena in the sense of being a
supporter of heros. The hero Perseus was ordered to destroy the
Gorgon Medusa, by Athena, who aided him with wonderful gifts
or weapons. In this sense Ariadne may be similar to the Welsh
Arianrhod (Silver Wheel) who is a supplier of arms in the
'Mabinogion', and a giver of names.
7 See Appendix III.
8 Fair Eleanor sat in her tower on high Sewing a silver seam. . . .
And there she espied a coffin a-coming,

The fairest that ever she'd seen. Child, 42.
9 Graves 1961: 107-12; Gantz 1976.
10 Stewart 1976 and 1985.
11 Burnham, J. M. 1908; Murray, J.A.H. 1875; Child, number 37.

APPENDIX I

1 *The Prophecies of Merlin* (verse 93).
2 The text proceeds with details of manifestation and individuation, finally reaching particular fishes, birds, and specific geographical locations.

We find this very theme repeated in the seventeenth century by the Reverend Robert Kirk, who argued that the existence of Fairies and the Second Sight was of the Third Order of spiritual beings, similar to the daemons described above. Kirk states that one of the tenets of the fairy people is 'That nothing perisheth, but (as the Sun and Year) everie thing goes in a Circle, Lesser or Greater, and is renewed and refreshed in its revolutiones, as 'tis another, That Every Body in the Creatione, moves, (which is a sort of Life:) and that nothing moves but what has another Animall moving on it, and so on, to the utmost minutest corpuscle that's capable to be a receptable of Lyfe.' Kirk, *The Secret Commonwealth*, 1692.

Bibliography

Allen, Richard Hinckley, *Star Names, Their Lore and Meaning*, New York.

Apuleius. *The Golden Ass, De Deo Socratis* various translations.

Bailey, A. *Esoteric Astrology*

Baldwin, C. S. (1914), *An Introduction to Medieval Literature*, New York.

Belden, H. M. (1911), 'The Relation of Balladry to Folklore'. *Journal of American Folklore*, vol. XXIV.

Boswell, J. (1941), *The Journal of a Tour to the Hebrides with Doctor Samuel Johnson*, London.

Bouchet, P. *Science et Philosophie des Druides*, Drancy.

Brennan, M. (1983), *The Stars and the Stones*, London.

Burnham, J.M. (1908), 'A Study of Thomas of Erceldoune', Publications of the Modern Language Association, vol. XXIII.

Campbell, J.F. (1860), *Popular Tales of the West Highlands*, Edinburgh.

Campbell, J.G. (1902), *Witchcraft and Second Sight in the Highlands and Islands of Scotland*, Glasgow.

Carmichael, A. (1928), in Watson (ed.), *Carmina Gadelica*, Edinburgh.

Cheetham, E. (1973), *The Prophecies of Nostradamus*, London.

Child, F.J. (1892-8), *The English and Scottish Popular Ballads*, Boston.

Clodd, E. (1920), *Magic in Names*, London.

Coleman, J.C. (1964), *Abnormal Psychology and Modern Life*, Illinois/London.

D'Arbois, H. (1906), *Les Druides et les dieux Celtiques à formes d'animaux*, Paris.

Davidson, H. (1971), *The Journey to the Other World*, Folklore Society.

Davis, E. (1804), *Celtic Researches*.

Dunn, J. (1914), *Tain Bo Cualnge* (Translation).

Dyer, T.F. Thistleton (1883), *Folklore of Shakespeare*, London.

Eliade, M. (1964), *Shamanism, Archaic Techniques of Ecstacy* (trans., W. Trask), New York.

Evans, J.G. (1887), *The Text of the Mabinogion from the Red Book of*

Hergest, Oxford.

Evans, J.G. (1906), *The Black Book of Carmarthen*, Pwllheli.

Evans, J.G. (1907), *The White Book Mabinogion*, Pwllheli.

Evans, J.G. (1910), *The Book of Taliesin*, Llanbedrog.

Evans, S. (trans.) *The History of the Kings of Britain* by Geoffrey of Monmouth, London.

Evans-Wentz, W.Y. (1911), *Fairy Faith in Celtic Countries*, Oxford.

Evans-Wentz, W.Y. (1920), *the Tibetan Book of the Dead*, London.

Gantz, J. (1976) (trans.), *The Mabinogion*, Penguin, Harmondsworth.

Geoffrey of Monmouth, *History of the Kings of Britain* (see Evans, Giles, Thompson, Thorpe, for translation).

Gerald of Wales, *The Journey through Wales/The Description of Wales*

Giles, J. (1896), *The History of the Kings of Britain*, London.

Godwin, J. (1979), *Robert Fludd*, London.

Godwin, J. (1979), *Athanasius Kircher*, London.

Govinda, Lama A. *Foundations of Tibetan Mysticism*, London.

Graves, R. (1956), *Pharsalia* (translation of Lucan), London.

Graves, R. (1961), *The White Goddess*, London.

Graves, R. *The Greek Myths*, London.

Guest, Lady C. (1904) (trans.), *The Mabinogion*, London.

Hartland, E.S. (1894-6), *The Legend of Perseus*, 3 vols, London.

Henderson, G. (1911), *Survivals in Belief among the Celts*, Glasgow.

Heywood, T. (1641), (1812), *The Life of Merlin with his Strange Prophecies ... A Chronographical History* (reprint 1812, Carmarthen).

Holinshed, *Chronicles of England, Scotland, and Ireland*, London.

Hull, E. (1932), 'The Hawk of Achilles or The Legend of the Oldest Animals', *Folklore*, XLIII, 376-409.

Johnson, S. (1775), *A Journey to the Western Islands of Scotland*, London.

Jones, F. (1954), *The Holy Wells of Wales*, Cardiff.

Jung, C.G., (1953), *Psychology and Alchemy*, London.

Jung, C.G. and Franz. (1965), *Man and His Symbols*, London.

Jung, C.G. and Wilhelm, R. (1965), *The Secret of the Golden Flower*, London.

Kendrick, T.D. (1928), *The Druids*, London.

Kirk, Rev. R. *The Secret Commonwealth*, reprinted Folklore Society, England.

Knight, G. (1978), *A History of White Magic*, London.

Knight, G. (1983), *The Secret Tradition in Arthurian Legend*, Wellingborough.

Lilly, W. (ed.) (1913), *Zadkiel: an Introduction to Astrology*.

Loomis, R.S. (1949), *Arthurian Tradition and Chrétien de Troyes*, New York.

Lum, P. *The Stars in Our Heavens*, London.

MacCana, P. (1975), *Celtic Mythology*, London.

MacCulloch, J.A. (1911), *The Religion of the Ancient Celts*, Edinburgh.

Mann, A.T. (1979), *The Round Art*, London.

Martin, M. (1703), *A Description of the Western Islands of Scotland*, reprinted 1934.

Matarasso, P. (1969), *The Quest of the Holy Grail*, Harmondsworth.

Matthews, J. (1981), *The Grail, Quest for the Eternal*, London.

Matthews, J. (1984), *At the Table of the Grail*, London.

Mead, G.R.S. (trans.) (1963), *The Hymn of Jesus*, London.

Murray, J.A.H. (1875), *Thomas of Erceldoune*, Early English Text Society.

Parry, J.J. (1925), *Vita Merlini* (translation and commentary), Illinois.

Patch, H. (1918), 'Some Elements in Medieval Descriptions of The Otherworld', Publication of Modern Language Association, vol. XXXIII.

Pennick, N. (1979), *Geomancy*, London.

Philpot, J.H. (1897), *The Sacred Tree*, London.

Ptolemy, *Tetrabiblos*, trans. Robbins, F.E. (1940), Harvard.

Ratcliff Barnett, T. (1937), *Border By-Ways and Lothian Lore*, Edinburgh.

Read, J. (1939/1961), *Prelude to Chemistry*, London.

Rees, A. and B. (1961), *Celtic Heritage*, London.

Reeves, M. (1976), *Joachim of Fiore and the Prophetic Future*, London.

Ross, A. (1970), *Everyday Life of the Pagan Celts*, London.

Ross, A. (1974), *Pagan Celtic Britain*, London.

Ross A. (1976), *Folklore of the Scottish Highlands*, London.

Sébillot, P. (1882), *Traditions et Superstitions de la Haute Bretagne*, Paris.

Sharkey, J. (1975), *Celtic Mysteries*, London.

Siculus, D. (1933), *The History . . .* (trans) C. H. Oldfather, London.

Spence, L. (1978), *Occult Science in Atlantis*, London.

Spence, L. *The History of Atlantis*, London.

Steiner, R. (1907), *The Occult Significance of the Blood*, London.

Stewart, R.J. (1976), *Where is St George?* Bradford on Avon.

Stewart, R.J. (1980), *The Myth of King Bladud*, Bath.

Stewart, R.J. (1981), *The Waters of the Gap*, Bath.

Stewart, R.J. (1984), 'The Grail as Bodily Vessel' (in *At the Table of the Grail*, London).

Stewart, R.J. (1985), *The Underworld Initiation*, Wellingborough.

Tart, C.T. (1975) (ed.), *Transpersonal Psychologies*, New York/London.

Tatlock, J.S.P. (1950), *The Legendary History of Britain*, Berkeley.

Taylor, R.T. (1911), *The Political Prophecy in England*, Columbia University Press.

Thompson, A. (1718), *The British History of Geoffrey of Monmouth*, London.

Thompson, Stith (1955-8), *Motif-index of Folk-literature; a Classification of Narrative Elements in Folktales, Ballads, Myths, Fables, Medieval Romances, Exempla, Fabliaux, Jest Books and Local Legends*, Bloomington.

Thorpe, L. (1966) (trans.), *The History of the Kings of Britain*, Harmondsworth.

Thorpe, L. (1978), *The Journey Through Wales/The Description of Wales*.

West, J.A. and Toonder, G. (1970), *The Case for Astrology*, London.

Wilson, D. (1851), *The Archaeology and Prehistoric Annals of Scotland*, Edinburgh.

Wimberley, L.C. (1959), *Folklore in the English and Scottish Ballads*, New York.

General Index

Index of Selected Prophecies